Stories of a Leland Family

John K. and Luella M. Van Raalte

Copyright © 2015 Roselyn Flannigan and Elizabeth Karen Clark

All rights reserved. No part of the publication may be reproduced, stored in a retrieval system or transmitted, in any form or by any means, electronic, mechanical, photocopying, recording or otherwise, without the prior written permission of the publisher. Contact the publishers via the Facebook page: Stories of a Leland Family, or at Vansgarage.com/StoriesofaLelandFamily

ISBN:1514147815
ISBN-13:9781514147818

Publishers: Roselyn Flannigan and Elizabeth Karen Clark
Cover Design by Elizabeth Karen Clark

ACKNOWLEDGMENTS

    This book is a family collaboration that drew upon the compiling and editing work of Rosie (Van Raalte) Flannigan and Elizabeth Karen (Van Raalte) Clark in transforming the many stories and pictures into a cohesive whole. Sara (Van Raalte) Leeland transcribed and edited Van's WWII tapes and provided material for Chapter 10, "Letters from Luella". Virginia/Jinny (Van Raalte) Logan, John D. Van Raalte and other family and friends provided editing, feedback and support.

    We also thank Evi Davenport for her thorough proofreading and Karen Cline for her transcription of Luella's song "Waiting for Tomorrow." Working together, family and friends produced this collection of Leland and Van Raalte stories.

Preface

1	Luella's Childhood	1
2	Good Times with my Brother Al	25
3	Diary of Luella Nelson	37
4	Moving to Leland	56
5	The First Van's Garage	68
6	War Years on the Home Front	72
7	Service in the Navy Seabees	84
8	Stories about the Kids	113
9	Halloween 1960 – A Dramatic Rendition	122
10	Letters from Luella: 1955-56	126
11	Leland Volunteer Fire Department	137
12	Defending the Flagpole	145
13	Why We Became Catholic	147
14	Boats and Boat Trips	154
15	Maryland Logging Adventure	175
16	Trip to Portland and San Francisco	180
17	Mt. St. Helen's Eruption	183
18	Our Adventures in Mexico	187
19	Letters from Luella: 1971-83	197
20	Boating at 80: September 1988	212
	Epilogue	217

Preface

Luella Nelson Van Raalte was a prolific letter writer, keeping up a correspondence with over 100 family members and friends. Some of the following stories are drawn from those letters, others are drawn from an early diary, her memoirs, her notes of daily events, and journals of trips taken.

John K. Van Raalte ("Van") didn't like to write, but he loved to talk and could easily be convinced to record his stories. Then Luella or another member of the family transcribed those tapes.

We are fortunate to have these recollections that vividly describe growing up in the early 1900s (Luella in Good Harbor, Michigan and Van in Holland, Michigan), marriage in Leland, Michigan during the depression, starting the Van's Garage business, helping to build the fire department, raising a family, Van's service in World War II, and travels in their retirement years.

As in any collection of stories, there are wonderful stories of events and interactions with family and friends that did not get recorded. However we believe these stories assembled and edited by their children are both a family legacy and a treasure to share with the community.

Chapter One

Luella's Childhood

Luella Nelson Van Raalte

It was May 3rd, 1909 - a time when the sweet scents and the freshness of spring should have arrived but instead the cold winds of winter had returned and brought with them a snowstorm. Also, that snowy morning Mother Nature brought into the world a little girl - namely - ME. Since my mother was 46 years of age and already had six children, I have the feeling I was no more welcome than the snow storm. However never in my life did she ever give me any indication of that; she was a very good mother. I've been told I arrived with a pair of lusty lungs. In those days there were no hospitals for a pregnant woman to go to, no doctors to consult. Her only advice was from older women, and when the time came for a baby to be born and labor had started, a mid-wife was called in to take care of the delivery. A mid-wife was any woman in the area who had special ability for this type of work and cared to do it. Her fee was small and she was bound by no legal obligations. In my case, my birth was never recorded; I discovered this only when I tried to procure a work permit when in my teens. I was definitely here in body but officially I wasn't.

My mother was born of German parents in New York City on Nov. 29th, 1863. Her parents (Christian and Salome Neidecker) came from Eichstetten, Baden, Germany in 1857. They lived in New York until 1864.

Christian Neidecker   *Salome (Bockstahler) Neidecker*

My mother, Louisa Wilhelmina (Minnie) Neidecker, and her sister Emma were the only two children who grew to adulthood. The three or four other children died in infancy. When mother was one and a half, her parents moved to East Leland where some Bockstahler relatives lived. They were unable to make a living in East Leland so, when she was three, they moved to Chicago. Christian Neidecker was a tailor by trade, and he collected junk as a sideline to make extra money. Even so, the going was rough, so in 1873 the whole family came by boat to Good Harbor where they homesteaded a piece of land and managed to make a living. [This property is on M-22 at about 1400 South Manitou Trail just north of Overby Road.] Grandmother Neidecker died in 1884 and it was my mother's duty to "lay her out" in her burial clothes; no mortician was around to do this. Then, until he died in 1894, my grandfather lived with my Aunt Emma who was married to Henry Brown and lived on a farm in Omena.

My mother remembered a happy childhood on the Good Harbor homestead. She and her sister, who was older, had only each other as there were no other farms near. I think there was a crude schoolhouse in the area, which they attended, manned by a not too literate teacher as I remember my mother saying that she knew more than the teacher, since she had attended a good school in Chicago.

The mail was delivered by an Indian on horseback and the girls soon knew him as a friend. This must have been a big change from city life for the whole family. At the age of fifteen my mother seriously injured her right leg. At the time, it appeared to heal satisfactorily, but a year or so later sores developed that continued. It was osteomyelitis, which of course no one knew anything about at that time.

Louisa Wilhelmina Neidecker Nelson and John Aaron Nelson

She was in bed a year and that is when she learned to do lovely crochet work. Some ladies from the Methodist Church in Leland came to see her and taught her how to crochet and also brought materials for her and later they helped sell her work. She suffered much from her affliction; it was necessary for her to bathe her leg and renew the bandages twice a day. The latter had to be washed and re-used. One of the effects of the disease was a shortening of the tendon that drew her heel up into an unnatural position and made walking difficult.

The doctor wanted to sever the tendon but she would not permit it. Another doctor did make an incision between the two sores on her foot (this was done without anesthesia); what he hoped to accomplish she did not know. What he did accomplish was more pain. She lived with this painful affliction all the years of her life and died on January 4th, 1948 at the age of 84.

John Nelson family, Luella front row on left (circa 1914)

At the age of 24 my mother married my father John Aaron Nelson and they had seven children, one son, Oscar, and six daughters; Alice, Alida, Amelia, Grace, Wilhelmina (Minnie) and Luella. My mother was a courageous woman. She had the staunch character that pioneers possessed. Her life was hard and filled with suffering but she didn't complain. She only asked God for sufficient strength to take care of her family, which meant a lot of hard work. There were no conveniences: the washing had to be done in a washtub with a scrub board; the ironing with a heavy iron actually made of iron. She had three irons and they were heated on the wood stove in the kitchen; she would iron with one until it got cool, and then take a hot one. Of course there were no "wash and wear" fabrics in those days, so with six daughters there were a lot of dresses to iron. Clothes had to be hung outside on clotheslines winter and summer. Yet she took time to read to us, and I remember with pleasure the OZ books and others that we managed to get somewhere. We all grew up enjoying reading. I also remember my mother staying up late nights to make a big rag doll for me.

Johanas and Alida Neilson, parents of John Aaron Neilson

My father was born in Hallands Lan, Sweden on February 24, 1863. It was very cold there in the winter, and he told us about walking to school and the snow packing down inside his boots. He was always very fond of horses and as a young man in Sweden he took care of horses. He dreamed of coming to America, and when he was 21 years old he finally had saved enough money to make his dream come true.

I regret that I have no records available telling of his feelings when he reached the U.S. He worked in Pennsylvania for a while in a lumber camp but I do not know how long.

Eventually he ended up in Good Harbor where he met and married my mother on March 27, 1887. My mother's father deeded the farm to my mother so she and my father had a place to live. After being in the U.S. two years or so, my father had saved enough money to send to Sweden so his brother Benjamin could come over to the United States. Uncle Ben was younger than my father by a couple of years. He came to Leelanau, married a Scandinavian girl Tina, and they had a family of five.

Saloons in those days were for men only and I well remember my father and Uncle Ben going to one often and over-indulging. Neither family could afford this strain on the budget but the men went anyway either to forget the problems of the day, or to prove their masculinity. In any case, once there, they threw discretion to the winds and became inebriated. Both families suffered from this. My father had a rough exterior but he was kind-hearted and would help his neighbors whenever he could. I was always a little in awe of him even though he was always very good to me. I remember one time in the winter after my sister Minnie had died, it had snowed and the snow was very deep, so he walked ahead of me to school to break a path and came to get me in the afternoon. It was three miles from our house to school through mostly fields and woods, only a short distance of it was on a traveled road.

Curly haired Luella on the Nelson farm

I grew normally, I guess, and my only affliction seems to be that since I was the baby of the family I was very spoiled. Believe me; I have been reminded of this many times by my husband!

Of early childhood I have only a few memories such as having the measles and having to stay in a dark room; of being put high on a haystack which seemed to be crawling with bugs and I yelled until someone took me down! It perhaps wasn't very high, and maybe there were only a few bugs.

Other early memories are of following my father down the road one day when he left for Leland with a wagon and two horses. I was wearing a big dark blue hat that I liked very much. Someone must have missed me and came running after me before I had gone too far. I remember being very afraid of men and hiding behind my mother's skirt whenever a peddler came, which was fairly frequent. I also remember turning the chairs toward the wall so that our neighbor Paul, who lived two miles away, would not come. I was small enough to imagine that this was some kind of magic that would work. I remember sitting in a chair sorting navy beans in the winter, so the best ones could be bagged and sold. This was usually done on very stormy days.

John & Minnie Nelson at their Good Harbor farm

Our home was built of wood and the outside had never been painted. There were four rooms downstairs: bedroom, living room, dining room and kitchen; and two small bedrooms upstairs. It was not very tight and in the winter it was cold. I remember looking at the beautiful frost pictures on the dining room window as I ate steaming oatmeal, our staple breakfast food. Of course, there was no bathroom. The outhouse was at least a hundred feet from the house, too far to go at night so we used chamber pots. The outhouse was set under a tree and when I was older it was a good spot to sit and read in the summer while taking care of my "daily duty", that is, unless a bee decided to come around. The toilet tissue of today was unheard of then. We used catalog pages, so wiped our bottoms with pictures of anything from machinery to wedding dresses.

Two steps down from the kitchen was a shed and this is where my mother washed clothes in the spring, summer and fall. In the winter she had to put the steaming tubs in the kitchen. She washed with a scrub board and strong homemade soap. There were two stoves to heat the house, one in the kitchen and one in the living room, both fired with wood.

In the wintertime my father felled trees, sawed them into stove length pieces, then split them into usable sizes and piled them into four-foot high, eight foot long piles. This was called a cord of wood. We girls usually helped with this. What we didn't use ourselves, my father hauled to sell in Leland in the summer time. He had regular resort customers to supply each year. Many times I rode the five miles to town with him sitting on top of a wagonload of wood. I could help him load and unload the wood. This was always fun for me.

There was no electricity of course. Our house was lit with kerosene lamps. When I older (9 or 10), it was my job to wash the sooty lamp chimneys, trim the wicks and fill the lamps with kerosene. This usually had to be done every day.

We had no telephone. No music either except for an old organ on which I played whatever I could learn by myself. When I was ten or twelve, my sister Alida gave us a hand-cranked phonograph with records. What a treat this was. All the records were played over and over. One record I didn't like was called "The Cowboy's Lament" [in which a dying cowboy tells his story to a living cowboy]. It made me feel very sad since my sister Minnie had died just a year or so before, and anything about death saddened me.

Our water came from a well with a pump so all our water had to be hand pumped and then carried 50 feet or more to the house. This also was my job. We had a fighting rooster and one day while I was carrying two pans of water to the house he attacked me! I threw both pails of water at him and ran. I was very afraid of him, yet when my father killed him some time later, I cried. He was such a plucky little rooster.

We had a big ramshackle barn, not very well kept, that housed three horses, "King," Charley" and "Don" as well as three cows, "Nellie", "Daisy" and "Black Beauty". There was an old buggy outside that I liked to play in with my dolls in the summer and pretend that we were going someplace.

Luella Nelson

An old corncrib was my playhouse and it was wonderful because it had a partition, so there were two rooms. Also, since the sides were slated, boards could be put in and corner cupboards made. Little housekeepers as well as big ones need plenty of shelves. I spent many happy hours in this playhouse, first with my sister and then, after she died, by myself. I would pretend I had company and carry on conversations with them. Sometimes it was very irritating to be interrupted to set the table, get water or to do some other job for my mother. Poor mother, I didn't realize then how hard it was for her to do all the work she had, and what a brave soul she was.

Religion and Church

My early memories of church are vague. I don't remember ever going to church in the wintertime, but in the summertime we walked five miles to the Pilgrim Holiness Church, sometimes called "the Kilway Church" as Mose Kilway owned the land and building and was a substantial contributor. I liked Sunday School and enjoyed meeting my friends there, Orpha Kropp and Alice Swanson. Orpha had older sisters and when she asked them for money for Sunday School they said, "Here are some pennies, honey" and I remember wishing that I had someone to call me honey.

I didn't like revival meetings though. The preachers would yell about hell and damnation and then walk among the people and urge them to come forward and confess their sins and be saved, less they died before they had another chance and be damned forever. Many people went forward to the wooden bench, knelt down, cried and confessed their sins. I knew I had lies to confess but was much too shy to go forward so I struggled with a guilty conscience and my fear of death became more acute.

Many times after my sister died I would wake up at night with my stomach hurting. I would wake my mother and she talked to me until I felt better. Actually it was not a stomach ache, but fear of death that troubled me. My poor tired mother must have had the patience of Job. I was afraid to sleep upstairs alone so my mother fixed a bed for me in the living room by pushing together a Morris chair and a captain's chair. Not too comfortable but at least I was close to someone I loved and who loved me. Those shouting ministers didn't know the harm they did.

We didn't really belong to the Pilgrim Holiness Church. My mother was brought up Methodist in Chicago, but there wasn't a Methodist church in Good Harbor. The nearest was in Leland, and because of her leg affliction that was too far to walk. My father would not allow the horses to be driven on Sunday since they had worked hard all week, so my mother was a Bible Christian. She read it faithfully, and many times I heard her praying, not formal prayers, but a personal prayer to God of thanks, and a plea for strength to do her job. My father was brought up Swedish Lutheran but fell away from the church when he came to this country. There was a German Lutheran Church in Good Harbor but he would have nothing to do with it, so he attended no church at all until his later years, and then it was the Pilgrim Holiness Church.

I hated to have Sunday come, because I didn't want to go to church. But there were nice moments also. I remember Howard, the grandson of Mrs. Kaapke (a friend of mother's) coming home on Sunday with me. He was my age so we had many things to talk about. We walked home on the road that was for horses and wagons or buggies; it had two deep tracks. We would make a bet on who could walk the longest in the deep tracks; the one who won would get the chicken legs.

My mother always had chicken for Sunday dinner. She killed, cleaned and cooked the chicken herself. I have vivid memories of squawking chickens about to have their heads cut off and the smell of scalded feathers still comes back to me. Sometimes Howard and I walked home on the beach of Lake Michigan, skipping along on the wet sand; usually we would take off our shoes and stockings and walk barefoot. There were so many interesting things to investigate that it is a wonder that we ever reached home. Undoubtedly, hunger hurried us along.

My sister Grace worked for Rev. and Mrs. Morningstar (he was the Pilgrim Holiness minister), cooking and taking care of the children. They lived at Schomberg Beach (now Good Harbor Beach). There were many houses and also a store there at one time as many large boats docked there. My father worked at unloading the boats oftentimes, but that was long before I was born. I only remember the remains of the dock piling sticking out of the water.

Luella on Lake Michigan Beach with friends

One day Grace took me with her to visit and play with the Morningstar children. I had on a gold bracelet that my brother Oscar, whom I dearly loved, had given me. When Mrs. Morningstar shook hands with me she saw the bracelet and said "When Luella gets religion she will have to stop wearing the bracelet." I didn't say anything in reply, but I made up my mind right then and there that I would never "get religion" if it meant giving up the bracelet! That is the only thing I remember about the visit.

A Birthday Trip

For my seventh birthday my mother planned a trip for the two of us. My father drove us to Provemont (now Lake Leelanau) with the horse and buggy where we boarded a train. What excitement! It was my first ride on a train and the seats were red plush. We were going a distance of about ten miles. When we reached our destination, Schomberg, we got off the train and stopped at the small grocery store there, which is all there was of Schomberg.

Postcard mailed August 22, 192? from Lake Leelanau to Mrs.A. Nelson, Rt#1, Box 50, Lake Leelanau, MI

The store was run by Ed Swanson and mother wanted to inquire if his sister, Nellie, was home. She was, so we started walking to her home. It was about a mile to her home, which was situated on top of a hill. A big house it was, but that is all I remember about it. Miss Nellie was very prim. She gave us a lunch and she and Ma talked and then we started out walking again. We soon came to the Hohnke home and stopped to see her. At this point I do not remember if it was Grandma Hohnke we saw or Mrs. Ben Hohnke.

After that we walked about 2 miles to the Fred Bockstahler home. Fred was my mother's cousin. His wife Ella was very heavy and her feet were crippled which made walking very difficult. She had four children and the youngest was about two years old, which was a delight for me, as I never had the opportunity to have a little one around me. She enjoyed it also. I remember she sat in a high chair and would drop her toys (can covers and spoons) on the floor and I would pick them up. I'm sure she was not accustomed to such service and was making the most of the opportunity. We had supper with them and also spent the night there. I remember the bedroom was so big, much larger than I had ever seen.

The next morning there was more talking and looking at the garden and chickens etc., and then we started walking again. After about a mile or so, we stopped to see Mrs. W. She and her husband had a big farm and hired help. Mrs. W. was walking around bare-footed and I looked askance at her dirty feet. No one in my family ever walked barefoot and I thought it very peculiar. Being in such a foreign environment upset me a little so I hung close to my mother. Then when the noontime meal was to be served and to which we were invited, in walked Mr. W. and three men. Men, the scourge of my life! I was so upset I started crying so we left for home. I think Mrs. W. gave us something to eat on the way. We had three more miles to walk and I don't remember stopping anywhere else. It was a memorable 7th birthday.

School

Since I was now seven years old it was necessary for me to start school in September. I think I looked forward to it until I heard who the teacher was. A man! His name was Harold Moukstad and he didn't know it but he was in for a very rough time. I was the only one in the first grade class (no kindergarten in those days) and I burst into tears whenever he taught me. Mr. Moukstad had to teach all eight grades so fortunately the time he had to spend on me was very short. While the other grades were having classes I could color, try to write and study whatever words I managed to learn between tears. Unfortunately for Mr.

Moukstad, but fortunately for me, he got sick around Christmas time and Effie Johnson took over the teaching. Now, I had no problem learning. Mr. Moukstad was well enough to come to the "Last Day of School" picnic. I remember how my heart sank when I saw him at Effie's house. He perhaps was not pleased to see this crying child either. I remember how Effie kindly turned my chair around so I wouldn't have to look at him. So ended my first year at school.

I do have many happy memories of my days at Star School. I remember playing games at recess and noontime with the other kids, building brush houses, damning up a stream. My sister Minnie and I walked more than three miles each way to school and back. My sister Grace graduated from 8th grade the year I started school. At one point in my schooling at Star School I had a harrowing experience. In the wintertime the boys who lived near the school would bring bobsleds to school and at noon about six of us would pile on two bobsleds and go sailing down the hilly road. This was great fun but at the bottom of the hill was a sharp turn that took much dexterity to navigate. One day it was very slippery and the sled didn't make the turn. I was on the end and when we were thrown off I hit my head hard on the ice. When I got up everything looked yellow and voices sounded far away. The kids helped me walk up to the school and I told the teacher, Miss Nelson, "I think I'm going crazy! I think I'm going crazy!" What could she do? There were no phones to call anyone. There were no cars to take me home, so since I could walk she asked an older girl, Mamie Schultz, to walk home with me. By the time we walked the three miles to my home, I felt fine except for a sore head, but poor Mamie had to walk three miles back to school.

Summers

Summers were happy, but often lonely times. My mother had a big vegetable garden and one day a week during the summer she drove to Leland with a horse and buggy to sell vegetables. It was a lot of work to prepare the vegetables since all the water for cleaning them had to be pumped by hand. She sold carrots, beets, onions, lettuce, etc. After the vegetables were ready she put the harness on the horse and hitched him up to the buggy. Usually we took Don, the brown horse, but one time Don gave us a bad scare. We had driven about two miles and as we came up "Hills" hill, a white canvas tied over a haystack caught Don's attention. He stopped suddenly and wouldn't take another step forward. Mother gave me the reins to hold while she got out and took hold of his bridle and turned him around. As soon as she got back in the buggy, Don took off like a streak of lightning for home! She had to unhitch Don and hitch up another horse, King, and we were on our way again.

Luella and her mother Minnie

I loved these early morning rides, and whenever I smell leather warmed by the sun I am reminded of these times with my mother. We would drive into the Indiana Woods in Leland, after driving the five miles from our farm. It was always lovely and cool in the woods and quiet. The only thing to be heard were the birds singing, the squirrels chattering, the creaking of the buggy wheels as they rolled along the dirt road, and also the zinging of mosquitoes, the only discordant note, and also biting one.

We stopped at the Blackledges, the Frank Balls, Dr. Ball, the McPhails, Mungers, Littells and Russells. Perhaps there were others but these I distinctly remember. Usually, they would give me candy or cookies to eat. I didn't look starved, but I had curly hair and blue eyes and was very shy, a combination which most Mamas seem to like.

I remember the Frank Balls very well. Mrs. Ball was a very kind person. Her youngest daughter, Rosemary (later, Mrs. Alexander Bracken), was my age but a little taller so I inherited some of her out-grown clothes. I loved her dresses, and because of her, I was the best-dressed kid in school. The McPhails were three sisters, older women, who lived together, and they always had peppermints to give me. My oldest sister Alice worked for the Littells and the Russells who were from Anderson, Indiana. Don't ask me why I remember that. Mrs. Russell told me that she would send me a doll that looked just like me, and she did. Her daughter's name was Sarah, so I named my doll "Sara" and determined to name my first daughter "Sara" if I married and had a daughter (and I did).

After all of the vegetables were sold we would drive into Leland, tie the horse up to a hitching post at the Leland Mercantile and buy a few staples that we needed. Sometimes we would get a ring of bologna that was a welcome change from salt pork and dried beef.

At that time the Mercantile, owned by Oswald Cordes, Sr. and Albion and Archie Lederle, was an old-time store with long counters at which you gave your order to a clerk who filled it. Crackers were sold from a barrel. Cookies were in big boxes on a rack and the clerk took out whatever the customer wanted. Cheese was cut from a big block. Practically nothing was pre-packaged. In those days, during the summer, the Mercantile sent a young man two or three times a week to call at the homes of summer resorters to take their grocery orders and then deliver them. At this time there were no electric refrigerators, only iceboxes that necessitated delivery of ice two or three times a week. The ice was cut in big blocks from Lake Leelanau in February or early March, sometimes as early as January, and stored in big barn-like icehouses. It was packed with sawdust between layers and lasted through the summer.

WWI

I was about five years old when World War I started in Europe. I remember my father anxiously waiting for the weekly newspaper to come so he could find out what was happening. I had a big book with pictures of soldiers, guns and battlefields, and I brought it to him. I couldn't understand why that book didn't answer his questions.

Later when the U.S. entered the war, my brother Oscar was drafted. He was married and living in Detroit. After a brief period of training he was sent to France. My parents were very worried about his welfare. How well I remember the day the war ended, November 11th, 1918. Star School was in session and the teacher got the word that the war was ended so she rang the bell a long time and we were all dismissed. I ran all the way home to tell Ma and Pa the good news but they weren't there. They were up in a field doing some fall work so I ran another half mile up to the field. They were so happy to hear that the war was over. My mother said, "Thank God it is ended!" Of course, it was months before we saw Oscar but he did arrive home safely.

Minnie's Death

My oldest sister, Alice, married Ray Hott about the time I was born and they lived in Boyne City. She had four children, Dorothy, Helen, Arden and Ivan. She and the children came home to visit us every summer and it was always fun to have company even though we did get into scraps some times.

In the spring of 1918 Alice's husband Ray died of diphtheria. It was a dreadful disease and no immunization shots existed at that time. There was an anti-toxin that could be given after one was exposed to the disease, so Alice and the four girls received the anti-toxin shots. In July they came to visit us.

Luella and her dog

My sister Minnie, who was 14, loved children and so she was always willing to take care of and play with the children. Dorothy and Helen were only a couple of years younger than I and we had a good time together. Shortly after Alice and her family returned to Boyne City, Minnie came down with a sore throat, which Mother thought was a summer cold. But it didn't get better so Dr. Slepica was called. He said it was a "Quincy" sore throat and he gave her some medication for it, but it still didn't get better, and she felt worse. When he came again there were white spots in her throat. She had the dreaded diphtheria!

Apparently one of the children had carried the germ. Minnie had shots of anti-toxin but it didn't help and after long hot days of misery she died on August 28, 1918. I was down at the beach that morning watching the cows. My father came down to where I was and he said, "Minnie isn't suffering anymore." I was happy, because I thought he meant she was better. Then he told me she had died and I wept.

We all had anti-toxin shots after her illness was diagnosed as diphtheria, so none of us (mother, father, Grace or I) got the dreaded disease. However, my sister Amelia, who lived in Leland, and who had come to see Minnie, came down with diphtheria and suffered paralysis of the throat muscles; but she lived and eventually the paralysis went away. She had a six weeks old baby, Helen, who had to be cared for by someone else so she wouldn't get diphtheria.

Our house was under quarantine and later had to be fumigated. This was done with formaldehyde and so we couldn't stay inside. We had to stay outside most of the day, and for food we had sweet milk and bread and butter, all of which was in the cellar. That night we slept in the hay in the barn.

Because diphtheria was a contagious disease there could be no funeral. I have a vivid mental picture of my father gently touching the coffin in farewell to Minnie as the undertaker drove out of our yard. A few months later a memorial service for Minnie was held in the Swedish Lutheran Church, near the Swedish Mission Cemetery where she was buried. This church only had a traveling minister who came about once in every six months. The service was held as soon as the minister came back to the church.

I missed Minnie because although she was five years older, she would share some of her secrets and plans with me, and we slept together. Life was lonely for me, as we had no neighbors with children near my age. Sundays were particularly lonely and I amused myself in the summer by swinging and singing in a grove of trees that overlooked Lake Michigan. My father had built a strong swing for us and both Minnie and I had enjoyed it. Another Sunday summer pastime was decorating my hair and dress with beautiful roses from my mother's garden and pretending that I was a pretty and well-to-do lady.

Watching the Cows

During the week in the summer time my regular job every morning was to watch the cows for a couple of hours. This meant watching our three cows either on the beach where they ate snake grass and other grasses or along the road where there was a lot of grass and undergrowth. It was fun watching them on the beach because I could build sand castles in the wet sand. I used stones for people and acted out stories. Sometimes, using a small board for a boat, I sent stone people for a boat ride and often they never returned.

Mollie, Ma, Luella and Grace

Sometimes I became so engrossed in my play that I forgot the cows. Fortunately for me, they were usually not too far away. I just had to listen for the tinkling of their bells. It was not as much fun watching the cows along the road. I usually read a book or wrote letters. When I was 11 or 12 years old I had six pen pals from other States. (Note: at the time of this writing in 1976, I still correspond with one of my pen pals of my youth. Her name now is Florence Halbe and she lives in North Dakota, but I have never met her. Through her and me, our mothers corresponded also.)

Back to the cow watching. Along the road the cows were very docile and nibbled grass peacefully. The only disturbance was an occasional car, which didn't happen very often since not many people at that time had cars. They didn't frighten the cows but I didn't want to be seen, so I would run into the woods and hide.

I well remember my first car ride. When I was about 5 or 6 the road near us was being repaired and my father was working with the repair crew. Mr. Henry Kahrs was the County Road Commissioner and he owned a Model T Ford. I told my sister Grace that I would like a ride in the car, so she asked Mr. Kahrs if he would take me for a ride, and he readily agreed to it. I was very shy about going when the ride became an actuality, and when Grace didn't come along I was really scared (remember I didn't like men). The car was noisy and went so fast! I had previously only ridden in a buggy pulled by a horse. I got very scared and started screaming and was so happy when Mr. Kahrs stopped where my father was working. Needless to say I didn't get a ride back home in the car.

Luella on the fender of a car

Poem Written by Luella Nelson about a Leland School teacher

One day Mr. Sells said in History Class
"It's no sir this and no sir that
You are much too small my little lass
Your superiors to sass."

Well I went back to my seat
But determined deep
Down in my heart
That my teacher I would defeat.

Well next day in our science class,
Mr. Sells as usual was stating facts
On how our body was a mass
Of cells like little sacks,

When I as quiet as could be
Said, "I beg your pardon but would you please
Explain that mystery
Again and I will ever grateful be."

Well, Mr. Sells, he turned around and he
Did look funny I must say when he
Asked me if his ears deceived
Or if I really did say PLEASE!

Luella's graduation picture 1928

Luella's High School Graudation Class, Leland, MI 1928
Luella is second from left, top row

CHAPTER TWO

GOOD TIMES WITH MY BROTHER AL

John K. Van Raalte

I was born in 1908 in Holland, Michigan. My brother Al (Albert) was born in 1907 and we grew up like twins. Mother even used to dress us like twins and we hated it. Dad took pictures with a big 9-inch square camera that used glass plates for negatives and among the pictures are some with Al and I dressed exactly alike. Of course that wore thin when Al and I were coming back from Sunday school and a lady walking behind us remarked, "Aren't those cute twins?" Well, Al and I made a big fuss, and mother agreed to dress us differently.

John & Al Van Raalte

Al, Dora & John Van Raalte

When we were living on 17th Street in Holland it was only about four or five blocks to Black Lake where Al and I always went fishing together. We would fish off the settling pond by the sugar beet factory, using setlines with a sinker on the end. We'd whirl the line around our head and cast it out and have four or five hooks on it. You could catch bullhead and carp. Al and I would sit next to each other, but Al always caught the fish. He would even take the pole out of my hands and catch fish with it. Then Dad got a rowboat and Al and I used to row to Pine Creek, about three miles, and fish. We caught blue gills and sunfish and perch. A little later on, Dad got two pairs of oars and Al and I would row the boat to Macatawa Park and Jenison Park and fish for Lake Michigan perch called "yellow bellies." That was about five to six miles each way.

John as a young boy in Holland

As we got older, we would hike to Macatawa Park. I remember doing this in both summer and wintertime. We'd carry a frying pan and some wieners and some bread. We'd build a fire and heat up the wieners and have a hot dog sandwich. Then we'd hike back home.

On one of the winter trips, when there was a lot of snow, we were in the woods back of the shore, where there was about a 60-foot sand bluff. So we went over to the bluff and thought about walking back on the beach instead of through the woods. We thought sliding down the bluff would be a lot of fun. There was someone else with us, so Al and he slid down on their butts. But, being the smart-ass that I always was, I considered the frying pan that I was carrying and decided it would be a lot better to slide on that. So I sat on the frying pan, and brother, did I slide! I picked up such speed that when I hit the bottom, I went end over end and wound up banging headfirst into the icebergs, which knocked me out. Al had to knock a hole in the ice and get some water so he could bring me back to. I can assure you that was a long walk home.

In the winter, we had ice skates and we made a hand-sail out of canvas that we got from the scrap pile at the sugar beet factory. I remember Al and I going out skate-sailing on Black Lake once when the lake was sheer glass-like ice because it wasn't snowing when it froze. We'd sailed all the way down to Jenison Park and were sailing back home, and the wind kept picking up, so we were moving fast when Al hit a rough piece of ice. The sail picked him up and took him up in the air, and then he came crashing down on the ice. We'd taken a sleigh with us, so I had to go ashore and get the sleigh and pile Al unto the sleigh and haul him back home. He survived, but he sure was shook up.

Al and John Van Raalte

In the summer, Al and I used to go swimming. We would row the boat across the lake on a diagonal and swim over where the water was a lot cleaner. On our side, the factories dumped their raw sewage right into the lake at the beach. That's what every factory did then. Al and I both swam on the way back across the lake, taking turns rowing the boat and swimming. We got to the point that we could each swim all the way across the lake (about a half-mile), which was quite an accomplishment.

Going to Work and Trip to Oregon

Al left school in junior high, and went to work in the furniture factory. I went to school until the 10th grade, and then I can remember Dad saying that I had to get a job too, that I was too damn smart for my own good, and we needed the money. So he got me a job at Bay View Furniture Company.

Bay View Furniture Co.

I'm not sure exactly how long I worked, not too long. Al and I saved our money and, with a friend of ours, Russell Risselada, we bought a Star car that had a 4-cylinder continental engine, four wheels with high-pressure tires (60lb) and a touring body. It was like riding on an iron wheel! We set out in June 1926 for Oregon where our grandparents, the Keelers, and uncles and aunts lived.

Transcription of the 1926 trip journal - Michigan to Oregon

June 1 It was raining when we left at 6:00 a.m., but it soon cleared and then the wind blew about 40 miles per hour. We got off the pike in Benton Harbor, but were only one block out of the way and so got back easily. Got off the pike in Michigan City, Indiana and had to inquire about the way. We were all balled up in Gary, Indiana as there didn't seem to be any road signs. Had to make three detours just out of Gary. Camped at Joliet, Illinois. Met a traveler from Portland, Oregon who asked us to stop and see him when we went through Portland.

June 2 We crossed the Mississippi River at noon today. Camped in a grove just out of Mt. Vernon, Iowa.

June 3 Met a fellow traveling in a Gray Motor car who stayed either just ahead or just behind us all day. Our Star car was nearly out of oil and when we tried to make a grade it got so hot that we had to put it in low to go up. Camped at Scranton, Iowa.

June 4 Passed through Omaha, Nebraska at noon. Camped at Duncan, Nebraska beside a graveyard.

June 5 Saw our first Air Mail Station at North Platte. Camped at Buffalo Bill's Camp.

June 6 Crossed the Nebraska/Wyoming line at four o-clock p.m. Hot all day and no punctures. Camped at Pine Bluff, Wyoming. Could see the mountains at Cheyenne, Wyoming from here.

June 7 We saw a locomotive with eight drive wheels just before we got to the point between Cheyenne and Laramie where the elevation is 8,835 ft. Saw the oil town of Paraco, Wyoming. Camped at Rawlins and had our first storm.

June 8 Broke the rear spring about twenty miles from Montpelier, Idaho. Did the work ourselves and used Ford spring parts repaired by a blacksmith. Camped at Georgetown.

Mountain switchback road

June 9 Camped in a back yard, where the fellow told us about the John Day Highway.

June 10 Camped at Fruitland, Idaho beside a school. Had our first flapjacks.

June 11 Camped at Ecoh, Oregon. Had to go all over the town to get a jug of milk.

June 12 Saw an auto destroyed by fire beside the highway. Went over the Columbia River Highway today. Camped at a place about 12 miles east of Portland, Oregon where we met a traveler from Detroit, Michigan. Whenever we met a car we stopped and exchanged information on the road we had just traveled.

June 13 Picked about two quarts of blackberries for dinner. Camped north of Roseburg, Oregon.

June 14 Arrived at our destination, Bandon, Oregon at noon and saw the Pacific Ocean for the first time.

It took 14 days to get to Oregon. We stayed there until October and then came back. I wanted to stay in Oregon, but Al wanted to go back to Michigan. Aunt Patty and Aunt Verona were two of the relatives we stayed with. Uncle Allen was about my age and Uncle George had a few cells missing! Aunt Verona had a 22 rifle and shot a squirrel out of a tree, which really impressed me. The Keelers ran a sawmill and Al & Russ worked there. I was too much of a smart ass and they wouldn't hire me.

John Van Raalte, Aunt Verona & Al Van Raalte in Bandon, Oregon

Al & John Van Raalte at the Pacific Ocean

We had a seven-by-nine tent which we would pitch each night. Unless you camped there was no place to stay in those years. Al and Russ would always pitch the tent and I would always cook. Once Al picked a city dump as our campground. We had a two-burner gasoline stove. We had a sheet of canvas that we threw on the ground and a quilt that mother had given us and that was it. Flat tires were a major problem; when we first started, we would wait until night to fix them, but then would end up spending the whole night on it. So we started fixing the flats as we got them.

Oregon to Michigan Return Trip

Made 120 miles the first day and camped at Crescent City, California. Made 133 miles the second day and camped at Scottie, California. Made 183 miles the third day and camped at Clear Lake, California way up in the mountains. Went up in second gear continually for fifty minutes as we left Clear Lake. Camped at Appelgate, California beside the railroad track, at what we called "Hobo Camp."

Star car by redwood tree in California

Saw the desert first at 2:00 o'clock Friday. Forsaken country all the way from Reno to Windover, Nevada. Where we crossed the desert it was 50 miles across and we were able to see the mountains on the west side from the east side. Had new gears put in at Salt Lake City, Utah. We had to do all the work of taking the car apart and putting it back together. When climbing the mountains on the east side of Salt Lake we had to refill the vacuum tank.

According to the road map it is 2,937 miles from Bandon, Oregon to Holland, Michigan. The Star averaged 20.5 miles to a gallon of gas and used 1 quart of oil to 18 gallons of gas. We never slept in a bed from June until we got home in October. Some of the places that we pitched our camp were really pretty rough. I remember camping above Clear Lake, California. We had pitched the tent after dark, and the next morning we discovered that we were laying not on the beach but on the rocks. They were any where from an inch to six inches in diameter. That was a long night.

John & Al Van Raalte

Misc. expenses on the trip from Oregon to Michigan:

Can opener	$ .05
Canvas	4.95
Pennant	.30
Spring (cut out)	.10
Tire patch	.35
Flash light batteries	.35
Paid out for Dip	.60
Curtains repaired	.40
Camp – Crescent, California	.50
Toll River in California	.75
Tire – Orich, California	13.25
Tire & 2 tubes – Williams, California	15.70
Camp – Nevada	.50
Camp - Nevada	.25
Camp – Grantsville, Utah	.50
New gears – Salt Lake City, Utah	13.10
Camp – Rawlins, Wyoming	.50
Grease rear end	.25
Alimite and tire patching	.75
Fuse	.10
Globe	.35
Valve cores	.25
Toll – Omaha, Nebraska	.25
Tire flap (when the rim cut the inner tube, the tire flap kept the main tube from being cut.)	.60
Pump hose	.20
Wreck	16.50
Camp – Dewitt, Iowa	.25
Toll – Mississippi River	.30
Tire – Chicago Hights, Illinois	9.00
Camp – New Buffalo, MI	.25
Groceries	31.50
Total	$111.10

Back in Michigan

When we got back, Al went back to work at Bay View and I got a job at one of the other furniture factories. At that furniture factory, I got my intestine punctured while working as a helper on the ripsaw. I pulled the piece out and threw it aside. I was lying on the floor and no one seemed to understand what was wrong. The man that did the crating was the First Aid man. I told him what happened. He found the stick. About 2 ½ inches of it was bloody where it had punctured me. They got me to a hospital. I remember that I tried to put my hand on a steam radiator to make it hurt instead of my stomach. I remember the guy next to me was hollering and the nurses told him to be quiet as the man next to him (me!) was dying and he wasn't complaining. I didn't know I had the right to complain and I certainly didn't know that I was dying! I didn't stay in the hospital long. They didn't do much to help me. I came home and my mother took care of me. I never wanted to work in a factory again.

Many years later, about 1934, after I had opened up my own business in Leland, Al came up and went to work for me. Al and I worked together for nine years. At first, he lived with Luella and me, and then he got room and board somewhere else. Later on, he married and bought his own house. We worked together until just before I enlisted in the Navy in 1943 and closed the business. Al got a job in the bomb-casing plant in Traverse. The war contractors were contracting for cost-plus-ten so, because good labor was hard to get, they paid good wages. In 1946 I came back and re-opened my business but there were quite a few years when Al and I didn't see much of each other. He was living in Silver Lake outside Traverse and worked at the cement-block plant.

After both Al retired and I retired in the 1970s, I had a 26-foot power cruiser, and Al and I took many trips together again. We went to Washington Island, Wisconsin; Escanaba and Beaver Island, Michigan; Little Current, Ontario, Canada and back. The last trip was one Al and I took with my grandson, JP. That time, we went all the way into Georgian Bay, up to Kilarney and through the Islands, and then back home to Leland. Then the trolling fishing got good here at Leland. Al was a good fisherman. We'd go trolling off from Leland or North Manitou, and he'd always catch the fish. We had a good time together.

John Philip (JP), John K., & Al Van Raalte

CHAPTER THREE
Diary of Luella Nelson

Editors Note: Luella was 21, working as the bookkeeper at the New Nicholas Hotel (now the Leland Lodge) and dating John K. Van Raalte when she wrote the following diary that covers the a year and a half from September 1930 through Christmas, 1931.

Nicholas Hotel, Leland, Michigan

1930 entries

Sept. 24: Went to Traverse with Van, Wilfred, and Henrietta Stander, to see "The Young Manhattan." We left Wilfred's car at the oil-station and walked home.

Sept. 27: Glorious! Our coats arrived and as if that weren't enough, Mr. Rosman [owner of the New Nicholas Hotel] said I might get off work to go to Chicago on the 7th. Isn't Life Grand? Went to Traverse in evening.

Sept. 28: No church. Cousin Rose was at Amelia's [Luella's sister]. I waited table. Helen [Luella's niece] and I got through at four. Van and I went to see "Good News." Had a nice time as per usual. Had a flat tire on the way home.

Sept. 29: Blue Monday, not so blue - just memories! Mrs. Safford left this afternoon. She is so sudden in her decisions.

Sept. 30: Mr. Rosman left early for Chippewa Falls, Wisconsin. I'm proprietress, a'hem! Oh yeah? (I always say that when I want to ridicule my egotism.)

Luella and Van

Oct. 1: Nothing much doing all day. Sorted linen and silverware; stayed at the hotel.

Oct. 2: It rained all day and the world seemed so dark and dreary until about five o'clock when the phone rang and "WE" decided to go to a movie, "Anybody's War," a darling story.

Oct. 3: A beautiful day.

Oct. 4: My last day of work - cleaned the lobby - and that's about all, stayed overnight at Amelia's.

Oct. 5: Did some work in the morning, attended church at 11; had dinner at home, drove to Glen Lake with Mrs. Schomburg and had a [tire] puncture. A kind-hearted Lake

Leelanau neighbor fixed it for me. Van mended the tire. I know it's done well.

Oct. 6: Just trotted around all day, getting ready for the trip. Went to Suttons Bay in the evening. "WE" went for a drive - watched the moonlight on Lake Leelanau. It was beautiful and we had a wonderful time.

Luella and her mother Minnie, year unknown

Trip to Chicago

Oct. 7: Left T.C. at 10:45 a.m.; rained all the way. Lunch at Baldwin (sandwiches and pie-deluxe), dinner at diner. Reached the city of bright lights about 10.

Oct. 8: Awake 8:30. Saw Oakwood Cemetery, Jewish tombstones and large vaults. Went downtown - shopped at Wieboldts. Mr. Clyde Mundue had dinner with us. He is from Cincinnati. Wrote mother, Lucille, and Van. Met Clarence Heath.

Oct. 9: In p.m. went with Mrs. S. and Mrs. Neuneister to Lake Shore drive. Saw part of floats in Chicago Day Parade, Planetarium, and Lincoln Park Animal House. Saw African gorilla, orangutan - Borneo Sumatra-Guereza Mendeley baboon. One put lettuce leafs on his head - acted so human. No wonder scientists think we are descendants of apes. But the likeness is there just to test man's faith. Saw small aquarium. Went shopping in North Chicago. Saw so many large apartment houses - almost broke my neck trying to see the top of them. So many people, all in such a big hurry and in spite of them all, you feel you're all alone, because you are just an atom of no more importance than one of the leafs on a tree and no more attention would be paid you if you fell by the wayside than would be given a fallen leaf. I'm not lonesome and I'm having a good time; nevertheless, I shall be glad to get back to dear old Leland and the folks and friends who love me and are interested in my life. The Schomburgs are so good and nice to me, and I like them all. Well, Diary dear, it's almost time for Supper and I'm starved after my full afternoon. I'll tell you some more later. Wish me happy dreams tonight. I have been having such terrible ones. Oh, I forgot to tell you, today's Chicago Days Parade was also given in honor of the big Chicago Fire of long ago - the one mother saw.

11:45 p.m. Just came back from the Tivoli [Theater] on Cottage Grove; saw Ruth Chatterton and Clive Brook in "Anybody's Woman." It was very good - something like "Common Clay." Also saw Frankie Masters and His Orchestra. Heard a marvelous piano solo; saw some beautiful stage settings and scenes. Saw Chicago's "I will" statue in Jackson Park. And now for Dreamland. Goodnight, Diary.

Oct. 10: Started out at 10; went through colored section of town; saw Metropolitan Life Insurance Co., also Courthouse. Went to Palace Theater; saw Richard Arlen in "The Santa Fe Trail;" very exciting. Also saw Olsen and Johnson in Vaudeville-Theater; all marble - very beautiful. So much expense for pleasure; I wonder if the same interest would be given to God's House. Man can make beautiful structures, but they cannot equal the beauty of nature. Went to Marshall Field's - magnificent! Saw lunchrooms, beautiful decorations. Oh! There are so many pretty things. My two poor eyes couldn't see everything. Went from there to Woolworth Building and had lunch and then to Denizens store. I had heard so much about the "Loop" and today I saw it. It's surprising how each person of the millions goes around minding his own business. I would be so bewildered by it all. Right now in the bedroom I can hear cars, streetcars rushing, a train, a policeman's shrill whistle, and so many people talking loudly in the street, somebody's radio across the street. I shall be rather glad when I can again hear just the waves of Lake Michigan and when all about me shall be just the quietness and the peacefulness of the night. I am looking forward to another night when "WE" can see and hear our Lake Leelanau. That doesn't mean that I'm not having a good time, Diary, because I am. I just want you to know that I prefer the country to the city. Mr. Mundue and a Mrs. Bowdner were here for dinner tonite. Mrs. Schomburg and I went to see the Conweilers and the Heaths tonite. I met a Jack Roberts also, and what do you suppose, Diary, the other evening when Mr. Heath was here, he thought Mr. Mundue and I were a young married couple. Isn't that a joke? I'm so glad it isn't true because he isn't like my ideal sweetheart at all!

Oct. 11: Got up at 9 and fussed around until 12:00 when Mrs. S. and I went downtown to the Shedd Fish Aquarium. So many strange European fish; took us an hour to go through it. Then went to [Field] Museum; saw all sorts of strange architecture and art. Saw Egyptian mummies. Mercy! How can anyone get a kick out of digging up those old corpses! Diary, it gave me the shivers just to look at them. We had lunch right there and then went to one of the halls to listen to a lecture on the primitive tribes of Angola, Portuguese West Africa, given by Mr. Wilfred D. Hambly. There were pictures with it and it was very enjoyable. The lecturer said that once while on his trip, he met a native woman of Africa smoking a pipe; he asked for it, wishing to buy it. She gave it to him and immediately went to get her mother; he found that he had offered her a proposal of marriage by asking for the pipe - and the lady was willing. He didn't say how he got out of it. Strange, isn't it? I'm glad we don't do that here. After that we went through the Stevens Hotel, also the Congress Hotel and the Blackstone. They are all so elaborate and expensive - beautiful dining rooms. Went window-shopping. Also went to a large store and went up and down on the moving stairway - rather thrilling. Came home at about 8. Oh! Both of us so tired - had supper and went to bed and dreamland. Oh yes. I sent thirteen cards yesterday - also wrote mother and Mary Lasky.

Oct. 12: Went to Chicago University Chapel at 11 - church will seat two thousand. Minister had a very good sermon; "Take my yoke, it is easy." Went all through church - very beautiful services, almost like ours. Well, Diary, since I wrote that last, quite a lot happened. We had dinner and by the time we had the dishes finished it was 3:30. We went down town in the car and left Mrs. Schomburg at the elevated. She was going to Milwaukee overnight to a friend's funeral. Then we went to the Sherman House and picked up Mr. Mundue; we then drove out to Oak Park. On the way I saw the Jackson Park Coast Guard Station where Henry used to work. We reached Oak Park, but didn't know where 723 Linden Ave. was (where Dorothy works). We asked one man and he said to go three blocks north. Well, when we went a ways and didn't find it, we asked someone else. He said "Oh! You're way off, go back about six blocks, etc. etc." Well we asked about a half dozen different people before we did find it. Dorothy was so surprised. She looks very well. We drove back and went to, guess where, Diary? I'll tell you, "The Original Coffees," Dan's nightclub. It wasn't half as bad as I thought it would be; we had sandwiches and fruit punch. The orchestra was good and we danced some. Mr. Mundue is a good dancer. So many young boys and girls were there and they all smoked. We left about 12 and got home at about 1 a.m.. I went to bed immediately.

Oct. 13: I helped Mrs. S. in the morning. Had a lettuce-tomato sandwich at noon. In p.m., we went marketing and came home and got dinner. Howard has a cold. We were all tired so stayed home.

Oct. 14: Another eventful day, Diary. We started out about 12:30 and took the streetcar to Archer Avenue and 22nd, the place where mother used to live 56 years ago. Her house is no more; everything is dilapidated looking. There are many Italians living there. Then we went to Chinatown and what an interesting place. We shopped in several stores. They have the most delightful things. I bought a darling pin for mother, a three-monkey ashtray, a crumber and two back-scratchers. The Chinese are so courteous and considerate. If I <u>wanted</u> to pick up a sweetheart <u>in Chicago</u>, I should get a Chinaman. But I'm not looking for any. Then we went to the Huey-San Chop Suey Restaurant. It is an adorable place. We had one order of "Chow Mein" but it was impossible to eat it all. Also we had some delicious tea in real Chinese cups. We watched some Chinese eat with chopsticks; it takes skill to manipulate them. They kept reaching in a large center bowl for portions of food and then would dip it in some oil. We asked a little four-year old Chinese boy if we could take him with us and he said "ung" very emphatically, which meant "no!" He was a sweet little youngster and said "Good-bye" to us. The waiter gave me a menu for a souvenir. I took some pictures, and we went past the Italian Markets on our way home. They have all their vegetables and fruit in the street. I liked watching them. One man was pressing grapes and he gave us some grape juice. Then we came home. Oh, by the way, Diary, the chow mein was made of noodles, chicken, Chinese potatoes, celery, onions, mushrooms and smoked pork. It was so tasty. I don't like the mailman here. He didn't bring any letters and I wanted one today. I was so glad to get mother's yesterday. Perhaps I shall forgive him, if he brings me one tomorrow. Well, Diary, I'm tired, so, you know what follows.

Oct. 15: Well, Diary, Old Top, I feel as cross as two sticks tonight. But one, two, three, let's smile. What's the use of letting everyone know you feel blue. It's rather nice to tell someone though. I won't say anything about the mailman because that arouses my ire, not at him though. He can't bring letters if no one writes them. Well, we went to the Flair stores, through the Post office, and Continental building; then through the Palmer House. We met Dorothy at Marshall Field's at three, then waited an hour for her friend who didn't come. We went to Woolworth's and to the Boston Store. Talk about people; there were just mobs and mobs. Dorothy and I almost got lost and, oh Diary! I'm so happy, I got my "Robin's in the Woodland." It's so pretty; I got it at Ryan's and Healy. We had a delicious dinner. Dorothy was with us; she left for home at 8:40. It will be her first experience traveling alone at night. I'm tired and I want to write some letters so I shall say, sweet dreams for tonight.

Oct. 16: Got up rather late as per usual. Mrs. Schomburg, Mrs. Neumeister and I went for a drive. Went through Washington and Jackson Parks and saw the Statue of Life, also the conservatory of flowers. It rained quite hard. Had supper at Mrs. N.'s. They have a darling apartment, way up in a Hyde Park Apt. Hotel. Also met Leslie, her son. He is very interesting; awfully funny too. We had corned beef and cabbage and apple pie. Mrs. N. is so nice. After supper she and Mrs. S. sewed on pillows and I read. Leslie took us about a mile and a half to a Cottage Grove streetcar, which we almost missed, and we took it the rest of the way home. It was 12:05 a.m. by that time and we went to sleep about 1 a.m. Got letters from Mother, Van, and Mary.

Oct. 17: No one in the house but ourselves, so we slept until after ten, had breakfast at twelve, then dressed and started downtown. Oh! but it was cold and windy on Michigan Avenue. We went up thirty-five stories in the Pure Oil Building, what a thrill! We looked out the windows - Michigan Ave. below seemed like a ribbon and the buses and cars on it seemed like toys. The river right below was green and angry looking, and we saw the new bridge that is being built across it. Also I saw the Tribune Tower, Mather Tower, Palmolive Tower, which has the powerful Lindbergh Beacon Light. And away in the distance is the majestic Lake Michigan. Then we went down. Oh! So fast it almost took my breath away, but it was lots of fun. Met Dick Morey at P.O.B. and also met Marie Leiner who sends us cretonne patches. Then we went shopping at Woolworth's for awhile and at the "stop and shop" market. It was a very attractive and neat place. At about 6 p.m. we went to the Avalon Theatre. It is perfectly darling, although it is small. For a ceiling it has a sky with twinkling stars and drifting clouds. We saw "Matrimonial Beds" which was funny and yet a tragedy. Also "Africa Speaks," a picture of an Englishman's expedition in Africa. It was very exciting. After it was over, we went home (about 9 p.m.) and had our supper. We were both nearly starved. My last night!

Oct. 18: Got up rather early for me. Packed the rest of my things and had breakfast. Then we took a car to 63rd and changed to one for Levitt St. Now that it's really time to leave, I rather hate to go. Mrs. S. has been so nice to me. I like watching the landscape. So long, Diary, for awhile. I'm going to start train munching because I'm hungry.

Back Home in Leland

Oct. 19: Went to church in morning and took communion. Slept in afternoon awhile. Van and I went down to Peters and played and sang. I went to bed early.

Oct. 20: Went down to Amelia's to help her wash. She went to Traverse in afternoon, so I finished wash. Got home about 8:30 p.m.

Oct. 21: We washed at home.

Oct. 22: Ironed in morning. Don't think I did much of anything in afternoon. Van and I played cards at Stander's - had a very nice time. Enjoyed the popcorn.

Oct. 23: Did odd jobs during the day. At night we had "Lutheran Young People's" hour at the church. After that we played games.

Oct. 24: Cleaned some in morning. Took [niece] Marilyn wheeling in afternoon. At night we had a meeting at Bremer's; went with Rev. Schmidt. We all enjoyed it. Had apples, of course.

Oct. 25: Just the usual Saturday cleaning, nothing exciting until Van came at six and asked me to go to Traverse City with him. I left ignition switch on so coil melted; got home rather late. "Van" is so interesting.

Oct. 26: Went to church at 9:30. Had dinner at home. Mother, Louis [nephew] and I went up to Bernard's, but they weren't home. Stopped at Kaapke's. Van came up in evening and we played 500 rum. He brought me some books.

Oct. 27: Helped Amelia wash. She went to Traverse in the afternoon so I stayed with the children. They got home at about 7:00 p.m. Went home and to bed.

Oct. 28: Washed in the morning and ironed in the afternoon. Guess I just went to bed in the evening. Oh no, I went down to Marie's and talked over party plans.

Oct. 29: Didn't do much of anything; just rested up and did odd jobs. Emma popped in about 9 p.m.; she played cards with us. Let's have Emma teach us how to count.

Oct. 30: Went over to Mrs. N's; then Emma, Marie and I, with Dorothy and Elaine in the rumble seat, went to Traverse City. Came back after dark, ran into a snowstorm and couldn't see five feet ahead. Dreadful, could hardly stay on road. Got home all right. Played 500 rum in evening.

Oct. 31: Took Emma home in morning. Made a Halloween dress for Helen. Went to choir practice at night.

Nov. 1: Cleaned at home and at Amelia's. Baked a cake. Washed my hair. Marie, Edmund [Peters], Van and I went to the barn party at Bremer's. Had a nice time but felt blue and like a spoilt child. Let others see it - never again if I can help it, 'cause it caused a misunderstanding which came pretty near not being set right.

Nov. 2: Got up at 10:00 and went to church at 11:00. Saw Van. Had a lonesome dinner at home. Took the children to the scenic tower in p.m. Amelia and Henry went to Grants so I stayed down there. Van came over. I was *so* glad to see him. I enjoy listening to him. Got home at 2:00 a.m. Hum!

Nov. 3: Helped Amelia wash and cleaned the car with Alex's help. Got myself all wet in the bargain. Bud was down in the evening to see Dad.

Nov. 4: Washed in the morning; voted at noon. Went to Lake Leelanau this afternoon, and wrote a letter to Fred [Hahnenberg] tonite.

[No entries for Nov. 5 - Nov. 25th, 1930]

Thanksgiving in Holland

Nov. 26: Oh Glory! It's not storming! Van and I left for Holland at 7:00 a.m. Had a nice trip. Left Hanky at Grand Rapids. Terribly stormy between there and Holland; we had to stay behind a truck all the way because we couldn't see to pass it. We reached there about 1:30. I was so glad to meet his mother. She is exactly like he described her to be. In the afternoon, we went to see his sister Dora - and then we saw the resort.

Luella

Nov. 27: Thanksgiving Day! What a lot we have to be thankful for. I'm so happy - it's storming dreadfully but we're in Holland, so why should we worry? In the morning we visited the Bay View Furniture factory where Mr. V. and Al work. It was very interesting. Then we went home and had a big dinner. Washed dishes. I sewed letters on Van's B.B. [basketball] shirt. Then we had supper. After that we went to see "Three French Girls"; Reginald Denny and Fifi d'Orsay played in it. It was rather suggestive. We went home and talked awhile, and then we went to bed and sweet dreams.

Nov. 28: Got up at 6:15 when a beloved voice called "Luella." Said good-bye to Mr. Van Raalte and Albert. Had breakfast, then Mrs. V. and I chatted while Van went downtown. We left at 10:30, picked up Hanky up at G.R. and then went on our way home. It was very cold but we didn't mind it, because we have a ritzy little heater in the car and everybody was happy. Van bought us all a sucker, and a box of candy. We took some pictures on the way. Reached T.C. about four. I visited Mi Lady Beauty Shoppe. At 5:30, we met Wilfred at Pete's, had supper and then started out for Elk Rapids. The Indps. were to play that night. The game was exciting. Leland lost 17-20, but they sure were traveling fast at the end. We had an enjoyable ride home. That Thanksgiving vacation will hold many pleasant memories for me.

Nov. 29: The day following the nite and the nite before. No ambition at all. Getting a cold. Went to bed at 8:30.

Nov. 30: "We" went to church in the morning. I felt miserable all afternoon. Van came up in the evening and we played cards at Stander's. Heard "Just A Little Closer."

Dec. 1: Helped Amelia wash. Weather very nasty. Gwen [niece] stayed overnite with me. Wrote Lucille and to Chicago.

[No entries from Dec. 1, 1930 to Nov. 3 1931]

<u>1931 entries</u>

Trip to Lansing with Dad Nelson to see My Sister Grace

Nov. 3: Started for Lansing at 8:00; reached there at 2:00. Grace was so surprised. Visited rest of afternoon; after supper we played Euchre and then went to bed. Wrote Mother and Van.

Nov. 4: Helped Grace in morning. In p.m., we went through the Capitol. Grand! Saw all the relics in basement. Went downtown to several stores. Played cards again in evening.

Nov. 5: Same thing in morning. Visited school in afternoon - very interesting. Then we went to East Lansing on a streetcar; saw a lot of MSC [Michigan State College] buildings. It snowed and we got all wet and cold hunting for Arthur's [Grace's husband] car, and then had to wait an hour for him. Awfully glad to get home. Saw clock in East Lansing that cost about $75,000. A lot of money! Attended a prayer meeting at night. Very few there. Met Rev. Nelson and wife; they have the sweetest child.

Nov. 6: Took pies down to school in morning. Cleaned house a little in afternoon. Went through Reo factory and saw car being made. Also present when a new car was started for the first time. Mr. Austin took us through. In the evening we went to a kindergarten play; "Black Sambo" was dramatized. Afterwards we all played cards at Gen's [niece]. Enjoyed it very much.

Nov. 7: We hurried to get ready to start for Flint. Left about 12:00 and got there at 2:00. Aunt D. asked us for supper. Grace and family and I stayed overnite there. Dad stayed with Molly. Went to see Emil and Evelyn.

Nov. 8: Went to Baptist Church - didn't like it at all. Had big chicken dinner at Aunt D.'s. Went driving in afternoon; saw a lot of magnificent houses, but I'd rather have a nice little cottage. Saw the school for the deaf. Also went over some of Flint's worst roads. We had supper with Molly and then we went home to Lansing. Dad stayed on. He went to Detroit the first of the week. Guess he had a very good time.

Nov. 9: We washed because the weather was just grand; went for a walk in afternoon and met Mrs. Perry. Played cards in the evening. But, best of all, was a letter from my dearest in the morning. Also one from mother. I missed someone an awful lot. Mrs. Hultz had dinner with us. She has a sweet personality.

Nov. 10: Grace ironed in morning and then we cleaned. Right after dinner we went to see [Van's] Aunt Patty. She is awfully nice. Van looks like her a little. Then we went to visit Ada. She has a nice group of children. She showed us all through her school. City schools certainly have a lot of advantages. In the evening we went to Fritz Kreisler concert. It was great; he made the violin talk and everything.

Nov. 11: Helped Grace in morning. Molly and family, Uncle Ben and Dad came over for dinner. We went to see Retta, but she wasn't home. They stayed for supper. After that, they all played cards and then went home.

Nov. 12: Had breakfast and then Uncle Ben, Dad, and I started for home at about nine. Reached Traverse about 2:00. Alice [sister] was home, so glad to see her. Van came up at night and we went for a little drive after church. You never realize how much someone means to you until you are away from each other.

Home in Leland

Nov. 13: Slept until 10:00. Helped mother at night. Went with Van to B.B. at Elk Rapids. It was so exciting. We won 20-16 - Happy? I'll say so and proud too. Coming back we had Richard Wakulot, Betty Lamie, Dick Steffens, Bud Roberts, Flip Steffens, and Gerald Voice. The more the merrier and we were merry. Had a lunch at Pete's. Pie al a mode, and our stomachs didn't protest. We all acted sort of - well, just cuckoo.

Nov. 14: Took Alice to Traverse to meet an A & P truck bound for Boyne City. Cleaned in afternoon and went to bed early.

Nov. 15: Went to church in morning. It was good to get back to our dear old church. Had dinner and then Van took us all for a drive around Northport, Omena, etc. After that, "We" went for a "little drive," explored a new road...and it ended happily. Saw an owl. Then Van said, "Can you go to Traverse without a hat?" and I replied in the affirmative. So off we went. Had supper at Pete's and then saw the movie "Susan Lenox (Her Rise and Fall)" with Greta Garbo and Clark Gable playing, and then home. Another beautiful day to write down in the book of happy memories. Two pals happy and contented and loving. I pray God we shall always be like that.

Nov. 16: Helped Amelia wash. It was a very warm day. Didn't even need sweater. In p.m. we washed their and our cars. Quite tired. Went to bed early.

Nov. 17: We washed and right after the clothes were out it rained and rained and rained. So at night we wrung them through the wringer and put them on the clothes bar.

Nov. 18: Well, it's nice! Just worked all day. At night "we" went to Maple City to a B.B. game. Close game first half, but second - too bad. Score 16-28 against us. Lelandites are good sports though, and smiled right through. We are proud of their sportsmanship in a losing game as well as a winning game when they do their best. Afterward we went to Traverse and to Pete's. Van and I slipped out and went to Traverse Cafe to have some coffee and sinkers [donuts] - tasted good, even though I had to keep my gum under my tongue. "Had to" (I say) because my ma scolds me if I stick it in my hankie, and ladies don't stick gum under the counter. Went home (?). Yes, almost right away. The moon was pretty though. Anyway what's a few hours sleep more or less? We had Bud, Dorothy, Gerald and Marie Dennis with us the first part of the evening.

Nov. 19: Didn't do anything special during the day. Our new heater arrived. Van and I attended lecture in evening. After that played and talked. Got a letter from Grace.

Nov. 20: Cleaned woodwork in kitchen. Saw Dorothy and Lucille in afternoon. Wrote a letter to Mrs. Van Raalte and then went to bed.

Nov. 21: Just cleaned and then baked 137 cookies. Dad and I went to card game at clubhouse in evening and won a turkey. Nice, only I'm the only one that cares for it. We had a nice time. Did something that evening that all unawares caused a lot of havoc. People will notice things. But what do we care? Missed my better half.

Nov. 22: Went to church. I enjoyed watching Irene and her husband. Dad and I went for walk in p.m. Had supper, then Van came and we played cards. Took Dad home and then we had a nice chat.

Nov. 23: It's raining. Washed at home and left clothes in basket. Also washed at Amelia's and left clothes in baskets. Saw Mr. Rosman. Sent gift to chum. I'm looking forward to the day after tomorrow; hope it's nice.

Nov. 24: Dad and I went to Traverse. Got overshoes, stockings etc. Also got a finger-wave at Mrs. Lump's. Don't like her personally; she chatters too much. Terribly windy. Part of shop blew in. Zebra's played Manton and won.

Thanksgiving in Holland

Nov. 25: It's very nice! Van couldn't leave until noon because of complications at the shop. We left at 12:30, saw Ralph Firestone at Reed City, reached Holland at 6:10. Good to see them all. Had supper and talked for awhile, then "we" went for a walk. Came home and went to bed. We were both tired - Van especially so.

Nov. 26: Thanksgiving Day! And what a lot of things we have to be thankful for. We just got up in time to go to church -the 4th Reformed; very interesting sermon. Heard a Dutch song. Came home. Dora [Van's sister], Bill and children were there. We ate a big, big Thanksgiving dinner and then went for a drive to Saugatuck, Fennville, and other places. And then we had supper, although we all ate enough at dinnertime to last us a week. Dora and I played checkers that evening. Jack [Dora's son] is so darling, and so good. He is a real carpenter. Listened to "Amos and Andy" and then retired.

Nov. 27: Got up early (?) as usual. Had a quiet but nice forenoon. Went through Bay View Furniture factory in p.m.; also went downtown. Bought some "Dutch shoes" and "Goodnite Sweetheart." Had a chicken supper. Dora came over that evening and we had our pictures taken. Hope they are good. Then "We'" went to a movie. Saw "Flying High." It was awfully funny. Came home and went to bed, almost immediately. Our vacation will soon be over. Oh Yes! We had a lunch at the "Green Windmill." Van met an old friend of his.

Nov. 28: We decided to leave about noon for Petoskey. Had a nice drive but a tire went flat at Kalkaska. We reached Boyne City about 7:00. Van went on to Petoskey to see Stark, but he soon came back because Stark wasn't home. We played cards for awhile and then went to bed. Slept real well.

Nov. 29: Got up about eight. Went to church at 11:00. Heard an Assyrian minister. Had a big chicken dinner and then left at about 3:15. We had a lovely drive; it was a beautiful day. Stopped at Traverse. Got home about 6:00 and mother had a nice chicken supper waiting for us. The last of Thanksgiving Dinners? And our vacation is over. No need to say what a marvelous time we had. We shall always remember it.

Luella Nelson & John Van Raalte

Christmas 1931

Dec. 23: Such a hustle and bustle! So much to do. Practiced in p.m., made cookies and I played for school program in evening. Van came down afterwards. Children did real well.

Dec. 24: Busy all day. Went to Lake Leelanau. Church program in evening. The decorations were beautiful. Big trees covered with icicles shimmering in blue and rose lights, and garlands and wreathes. Van and I played "Santa Claus."

Dec. 25: Went to "Dawn Service" 6:30 a.m., then "we" opened gifts - and oh! Dr. H. Hatt gave me a pretty centerpiece, Helen S., hangers and napkin rings, Alida, dainty pink undies, Amelia, a darling "dance set" (pink), Grace, pretty hankies, Lucille, cute little doll mending set and a pair of stockings, Mrs. V., stationery, Shirley D., a nice vanity book, Mr. Rosman, a box of chocolate cherries, Mother, goods for a dress. And last but no by means the least, my beloved gave me a blue jacket and tam and stockings to match. It just fit and was I ever happy. He is so good to me. We then had breakfast. Didn't have dinner until 2:30. Then went for a lovely walk. It was such a beautiful day, no snow. Had a light lunch and played cards. It was a wonderful night, big full moon and all the stars. We have a radio on trial and we got some grand music. All in all it was a very Happy Christmas, almost too good to be true. And underneath it all is the thought of the true meaning of the day - "Christ is born."

[This is the end of entries in this diary.]

CHAPTER FOUR

MOVING TO LELAND

John K. Van Raalte

Choosing Mechanics - Cleveland 1929-30

After my rip-saw injury, I decided that there wasn't any future for me in the furniture machine room and I didn't like the finishing work on furniture using varnish and shellac. So I got to thinking about what else I could do and decided to go into automobile mechanics. I went out in the city of Holland and tried to get a job. The word was, if I was a mechanic, yes - they'd hire me; but if I was just beginning, they wouldn't hire me. So it led me to the conclusion that what I needed was to get experience. I read in the paper that there was an auto mechanic school in St. Louis and one in Cleveland, Ohio. Cleveland was closer, and it became a question of saving the money to go to school. At 22 cents an hour, that was a long process.

Finally, I saved up enough to pay the tuition, board, room, and laundry and took off on a train to Cleveland, Ohio. I got a place to stay that the school had recommended. One of my memories of that place was that it was owned by a widow of a police officer who'd been shot and she had two girls.

My first memory was of her sweeping down the stairs and that she had dustpans full of black dirt. The other impression that stayed with me was that the bed in my room was steel-framed and it was black and sticky. So I decided to get a washcloth and scouring powder and started to clean it. I found the bed-frame was white. The black was because the mechanics who stayed there never washed, and they got their dirty hands all over the place.

Van at left, at Foyes Garage in Cleveland

While I was in mechanics school, the Depression came along. Lucky for me, one of the instructors must have decided I was one of the brighter fellows; anyway, he got me to work on his own car. One day he told me that he didn't know for sure what was happening in the world outside, but he said "We haven't had anybody wanting a mechanic for a long time. There's a job that came in this morning, and you better go and take it." So I went in the office and got the job. I told the man that I wasn't finished with school and he said, "You can go back to night school," which is what I did. So I went to night school while I was working this job. I remember that the man I worked for had a garage, but he also had a bar and a house of prostitution next to his garage. All that was quite an eye-opener. Coming from Holland, with a church on every corner, it was a totally different world. It was during prohibition, and this man didn't pay off the local police, so the fellows came in and smashed up his bar. Then he closed his garage and I was out of a job. By that time, in the Depression, you couldn't buy a job in Cleveland, Ohio.

Van

So I packed up my car and headed back home. I drove all day and night and then slept for 24 hours. Then I got up and said to Mother, "I'll see if I can get a job." So I wandered around Holland, but I didn't get a job. I went north as far as Greenville, but no job. I got back to Holland and I went to a place where a guy was putting gears on flywheels. He said he'd give me a job, but only until he got caught up. So I worked a week. Then I took off again to visit one of the mechanics from the school who lived in Petoskey. His name was Stark. There were no jobs in Petoskey, so we got in my car and headed south. Nothing in Charlevoix. We got to Traverse City and I was told there was a man at Leland who had a mechanic quit. So Stark and I came to Leland and I stopped at the Standard Oil Station and one of the attendants said, "Yeah, he needs a mechanic, but the last guy quit because he couldn't pay him."

Well, I was still owed back wages from the guy in Cleveland, which I never got. Stark and I just went down and sat at the beach at the end of the street where Van's Garage is now. We talked it over and came to the conclusion that I would try the job for a week. I said to Stark, "I'll stay as long as he pays; and when he can't pay me, I'll quit." So Stark took my car and went back to Petoskey. I got a place to stay and went to work for Carroll Stander.

This was in July, 1930. The depression had just come to Leland. The banks closed. I remember that Luella's parents had some money in the bank and they lost all of that. But I had no place to go and had no money, so I stayed with the owner of the garage that winter. I worked for my board, room, and laundry, plus I got $10 a week. By the time spring came, I hadn't always been paid and I owed $80 for board, room, and laundry. But then in June, business stepped up and the owner could start paying me again. I stayed there two or three years.

As to what I liked about Leland - I liked being near the water. Lake Leelanau is 18 miles long and Lake Michigan is right there. So the water intrigued me. And I got to like the people. I never actually wanted to leave Leland. I did have an opportunity to go to work in Traverse at Cadillac-Oldsmobile at better pay, and I also was offered a job at Marshall Field's in Chicago after WWII maintaining their truck fleet. But I didn't want to leave Leland.

In my first years, I also stayed for a while with the Fred Perrault Sr. family, but I wasn't used to the kind of food they served. From there I went up to Edmund and Earhart Peters, who were bachelors, and stayed with them...maybe a year. Wilfred Peters was the oldest and he worked at the Print Shop, which was owned by Selby, who was Superintendent of Schools here. Wilfred ran the shop. He died only a few years later. Then I went to batching it in a house on the beach which belonged to the man I was working for; that was more or less of a disaster.

Meeting Luella

I was working at my first job in Leland, at the Carroll Stander garage, and a young lady (Luella) came down. As I remember, she had on a pink knit suit. Her father had bought a new automobile which she drove. The only cigarette I remember Luella ever smoking was the one on the day she showed up at the garage. Luella was working then at the New Nicholas Hotel (now Leland Lodge). She had started out dishwashing, then waiting tables, and wound up running the office.

Luella stayed with her sister Amelia, and her niece Helen Hott (later Helen Julerette) stayed there also. I called the hotel for a date with Luella and she said she couldn't go, but her niece would go. So I went to pick the niece up, and Helen was dressed in a green coat. I took Helen out two or three times and decided that was a flop. I tried again to get Luella out for a date.

I remember that first date because when I went back to Amelia's, the gal that answered the door had the same bright green coat on. Their voices sounded a lot the same, and I actually wasn't sure if it was Luella or Helen. We were going to Traverse City - in those days, if you had a date, what you did was go to a show in Traverse. I knew that Helen hadn't grown up in Leland, so on the way to Traverse, I kept asking who lived at particular farms, and the gal would always tell me who it was. We got as far as Suttons Bay before I said, "Well, you must be Luella." It turned out that the coat was Helen's but they were both the same size and they swapped clothing a lot.

Luella played the piano at recitals and played down at the women's club (now the art studio); she also played at church for the choir. She wasn't much on the jazzy kind of playing; she was better with hymns. Ernie Van Zee used to put on movies and Luella played the piano at the movies. That was back in the days of the silent movies. If you're not old enough to remember, there were printed words on the screen.

Once we connived a deal to go to North Manitou Island. There was a Model-T Ford at North Island. The gas tank for that car is under the seat. If you went up a steep hill, you ran out of gas. The way to go up a hill was to back it up the hill. When you ran a Model-T, there were three pedals on the floor. The left one was the clutch; if you pushed that to the floor, it was in "low". There was an emergency brake on the side that you let forward, then you let up on the clutch and it would go into high gear with a clunk and a jolt. The middle pedal was reverse. The right pedal was brake. We went across the island from the village to the west side, and on the way back we had to back up the hills, but we made the trip and had a picnic on the island.

One time, we went across iced-over Lake Leelanau with my car and we stayed overnight at a farmhouse because a terrific storm came up. I remember that an axle shaft broke when we started to drive out of the woods where the Ed Bremer farmhouse was located. Luella had decided that she wanted one of the kittens that was on the farm, so she put the kitten in her coat and it got excited and messed up inside her coat. We had to walk back to Leland across the ice because the axle shaft was broken on the car.

One thing I remember is that I got down on my knees to ask Luella to marry me. I also remember that when we got married, we had only $30. So we went down to Holland to my parents instead of having a honeymoon trip. The house on the beach where I'd lived as a bachelor is where Luella and I first went to live. We hung up sheets and blankets to partition off the bedroom from the living room. There was no bath, just a washbowl and toilet.

John K. and Luella Van Raalte, May 2, 1933

The 1933 wedding announcement was published in the Leelanau Enterprise:

> *VAN RAALTE-NELSON*
>
> *Miss Luella Nelson became the bride of John K. Van Raalte at a simple wedding ceremony performed Tuesday evening, May 2, at the Lutheran parsonage here. Rev. Edw. F. Schmidt officiated.*
>
> *The couple were attended by Miss Lucille Kolarik and Carroll C. Stander. The bride was charming in a becoming soft gray cape effect silk gown, gray crepe de chine hat with veiled flowers and gray slippers and gloves to match.*
>
> *The bride is the daughter of Mr. and Mrs. John Nelson, and is a popular member of Leland's younger set. She graduated from Leland high school in 1928. Mr. Van Raalte is the son of Mr. and Mrs. John Van Raalte of Holland, but he has made his home here the past three years, being in the employ of C.C. Stander Auto Company.*

After a few months, we moved to Greycote Cottage, where we could only live in the winter. Luella was pregnant with John and we only stayed there until June. We decided to move so we wouldn't have to move when John was born (in June). In those days, you didn't go to a hospital; the doctor came to the house. So we found a little house next to Elmer Dalton's that was owned by Elmer's mother, Annie. There was an outhouse and a hand pump. The winter after John was born was so cold and the house was so bad that when we put John in his highchair in the morning out by the stove, I remember the temperature in the room at the stove could be 110, and there would still be ice in the dishes sitting in the kitchen sink. The snow actually blew through the corner of the house, not the windows. It piled up in little pyramids on the floor. That was known as rugged living.

Annie Dalton decided I could pay more, and she raised the rent from $10 a month to $14. I remember telling her I would live in a tent before I would pay her $14 a month. Then I talked to Will Stander, who owned the house on Main Street next to his building. Now that was luxury. There was a bathtub, an electric pump, and an inside toilet. My, my, my, that was wonderful living!

Luella on porch of Greycote Cottage

Luella had a piano that came from the old dance hall, the original Riverside Inn. We moved the piano from her house to the first house (on the beach) when we got married. We moved the piano from there to Greycote, to the Annie Dalton house, and then to Will Stander's house. The next move we made with the piano was the easiest, because we bought the house at 411 Main

Street next to Will Stander's house. That house sold at $2,800, but the owner (Claude Kopke) wanted the payments to drag out, so we could pay by the month. I remember that we pushed the piano out on the sidewalk and rolled it down to the new house.

Riverside Inn, Leland, MI

Van Raalte home at 411 S. Main St., Leland, MI

John K. & Luella Van Raalte

```
Household Accounts for the year May 1st 1933 - to
                                                 May 1st 1934

                    CASH RECEIVED
DATE                               P      DR         CR

May 20  Wages                              5.00
    27  Wages                              1.00
        Total cash received       125      6.00

June 1  Wages                             10.00
     3  Wages                              5.00
     8  Tips waiting table                  .20
    10  Wages                              5.00
    11  Wages                             10.00
    12  Wages                              5.00
    17  Wages                             20.00
    24  Wages
    26  Wages (B)                          2.00
    30  Total cash received       126     77.20

July 1  Wages                     $15.00
    12  Wages (B)                          4.40
    12  Misc cash                           .50
    16  Wages                             10.00
    22  Wages                             15.00
    22  Cash back on Beer Bottle            .20
     8  Wages                             15.00
    29  Wages (B)                          5.00
    30  Wages                             15.00
        Total                             79.70  (fwd)
```

A page from the household accounts of Van & Luella, May through July 1933

CHAPTER FIVE

THE FIRST VAN'S GARAGE

John K. Van Raalte

John K. and Al Van Raalte, 407 S. Main St., Leland, MI

At the point, in 1934, when I figured out that my first job wasn't likely to last much longer, I made a deal with Willy Stander to rent the front end of his building at 407 S. Main St. for $10 a week. And I went down there and took my car and a bunch of tools and I was open for business. That was the first Van's Garage. I put a sign up front that said "Expert Mechanic." Well, nobody else knew the difference, and I had to bluff a lot.

By the time I started my own business, I was married and John was born. I remember the food in the cupboard was so short it got down to a box of crackers. Also, you have to remember that there was no welfare. I got Texaco gasoline company to give me one tank fill that I could pay off at 2-cents a gallon over time. The rest I had to pay for as I got it, which was tough.

Van next to garage at 112 S. Main location

The very first gasoline sale I made I remember very well. It was to Earhart and Edmund Peters, and I forgot to put the gas cap back on after I filled the tank so I had to buy them a gas cap. There was only 3-cents a gallon profit; so the profit from my first sale all went into buying that new gas cap.

You have to realize that I was an absolute stranger when I came to Leland. Nobody knew me and I knew no one. I only arrived here because I was looking for a job. Gradually the garage business picked up, but then along came the war. By 1943, we had gas rationing, tire rationing, and boy, it was tough! I went to the east part of the state looking for a job. I could have got a job in any one of the defense plants. Ford built a bomber at

Ypsilanti. But that meant I went back into factory production again, which I hated. It was the same thing over and over, day after day, month after month. I didn't want it. So I came back home and tried to keep running the garage, but I was working 16 to 18 hours a day (from 6 a.m. to 11 p.m.) just trying to make a living. I remember one winter day when I sold only $1 of gas all day. Finally, one day I came home and collapsed on the floor. Luella got me up on the couch, and Dr. Bolan came to the house and said, "You know, you're never going to work again. You're too far gone. You've got to do something about yourself."

But I had to work. I didn't have any income at all. I had a wife and four children to support. I was lying in bed and I got hold of the newspaper and it said that they were forming a new section of the Navy called the Seabees (C and B for "Construction Battalion") and that they were looking for mechanics. So I packed a bag and went to Detroit. I got a physical and they said, "You're in." At that point, they would take you if you were breathing. I weighed 129 pounds when they measured me for two suits of khaki, two of white, and two of blue. As I got back to normal weight, none of them fit. They all had to be let out. Anyway, they said they'd make me a chief at first-class rank.

I came home and finished up my affairs, built a building and put all the equipment I owned into the building and then packed my suitcase and went back to Detroit. They gave me the chief ranking and told me to come back in seven days. I said, "I'm broke. I want to go in right now." So I and six other fellows went out in the hall and held up our hands and we were sworn into the Navy. I suddenly realized that all my life as a civilian was gone. I was now in the Navy.

Editors Note: Unfortunately Van and Luella didn't record the many stories of the people and adventures at Van's Garage business over the years but "Van's" was clearly at the center of family life. The reproduction above is of a painting done in 2001 by Fred Petroskey and is used with permission of its owner, Van's Garage, Leland, MI. It shows the four generations of John Van Raaltes: left to right, John Philip (JP), John Henry, John Kenneth and John Duane Van Raalte.

Van's Garage is now is in its 3rd generation of ownership and 9th decade of existence. John Kenneth started the business as described in these memoirs with Luella working in the office and doing the accounting. Son John Duane worked in the business from an early age and took over the business in the 1960s. In 2005 John D. semi retired (he still works there part time) and turned control of the business over to his son John Philip (JP). Both John D's wife Jan and JP's wife Tracy have continued Luella's legacy of partnership in the business by handling the office and the accounting for their husbands. John K.'s great-grandson John Henry has also learned mechanics and works there when on break from college. In each generation, many of the daughters and granddaughters in the family were also involved in the office side of the business while growing up. Van's has recently added an expertise in vintage/antique car restoration to their services.

CHAPTER SIX

WAR YEARS ON THE HOME FRONT: 1943-45
Luella M. Van Raalte

The disaster and shock of December 7, 1941 affected our small family as it did everyone in the U.S. At the time we were renting a garage building, actually part of a marina, at 407 S. Main St., from Will Stander. When Van first came to Leland in 1930, he worked for Carroll Stander, a brother of Will Stander, in the garage which is now ours at 112 S. Main St. December 7, 1941 was a Sunday, and Van was alone at the shop (which he kept open 7 days a week and 15 hours a day). His brother Al was working for him at that time, having come to Leland in 1936. When I took his lunch to him on that fateful day, he told me what he had heard on the radio. We just couldn't believe it!

It didn't make too much difference in our lives right away, but eventually there were shortages, gas rationing as well as sugar rationing, and of course the government drafted all eligible men. We had three children, John, Sara, and Nora, and one on the way, so Van was not eligible for the draft, but he began toying with the idea of joining the Army Engineers and got information on it.

Luella Van Raalte

Then he heard about the "Seabees," a newly organized Navy Group, similar to the Army Engineers and in early 1943 he decided that he would enlist in the Seabees.

There was a lot of stress and strain involved in operating a business with almost no available help. Twenty five percent of the available men left Leland and went into war materials production. After Al married and moved to Traverse City, the restrictions against transportation became so severe Al got a job in a bomb casing plant in Traverse City. The strain of operating the business became too great and Van suffered. His weight went down from 148 to 129 pounds. After he became well enough, he decided to go to Detroit, the enlistment center. His thinking was "If you can't lick 'em, join 'em."

So we started the process of closing the business which was a tremendous job and, for one thing, necessitated the building of a temporary building on our property to house all the garage equipment and supplies, since we didn't want to continue renting the Stander building while Van was in the service. The temporary building, with all its interesting items, was a special delight for Johnny, 9, while Van was away.

I was very pregnant with our fourth child at the time and had very mixed emotions about the whole project. I was proud of my husband for wanting to serve his country but frightened at the prospect of having the total responsibility of the home and four children. Johnny was 9 years old, Sara was 6, Nora 4, and Virginia (also called Jinny) was born in June 1943.

On July 2nd, Van had to go to Detroit for a final briefing and induction. I remember his calling that night and saying "Well, Kid, this is it. Once I hold up my hand and say 'I will,' there is no turning back." He came back home for a few days to pick his clothes, and then was scheduled to leave by bus from Suttons Bay to Detroit.

He was sworn in as a Chief Petty Officer, so was put in charge of the trainload of recruits. He had asked Ernie Van Zee to drive him to Suttons Bay, knowing how hard it would be on me emotionally. So began 2 ½ years of separation.

He was sent to Camp Peary, Virginia, for his boot training. The boot camp training was by Marines and was rugged. Van, who was run down physically and emotionally, found it especially rugged. He remembers an ex-professional boxer from Chicago (broken nose, cauliflower ears) crying tears with his arm around Van, telling him he wanted to go home. He was in Van's platoon. He was punch drunk and emotionally unfit for service. Van had him mustered out. Another young man had fits during the night. He would bang his head on the floor until it was bloody. He

Chief Petty Officer John K. Van Raalte

wanted to stay in and he bawled like a baby when Van told him he was going to muster him out.

On the home front, it was rugged also, but in a different way. Four children, one a new baby, kept me busy, but how I missed my husband! He wrote faithfully, almost every day, and telephoned when he could. In early August, he had a three-day leave and was invited to the home of Mark Bogar (his buddy) in Selinsgrove, PA. He wanted me to come there, and how I wanted to go also. But plane reservations were not available, and I was nursing Jinny, so would have had to take her. Train transportation was too erratic, so it was impossible for me to go. I kept hoping that maybe somehow, some way, a Navy plane could bring him to Traverse, but no such luck. So we didn't see each other until October, when he had a 10-day leave. He took a train to Holland and I drove to Holland with the four kids in our old Buick to get him. Alice, a teacher from Holland who was teaching at Leland school, drove down with me, which was a big help as Jinny was only four months old at the time. The ten days went much, much too fast, and all too soon, he had to board a train out of Traverse for Camp Peary.

Coming home that night to a lonely, dark house was one of the darkest days of my life. But time rolls on, and my days were filled with all of the work involved with the children, laundry, school lessons, illnesses, etc. I missed the bookkeeping for the business. I wrote Van daily to keep him up on home activities. Shortly after Van's leave in October, his group was transferred to Camp Davis, RI, and Navy life became more bearable, as they were through with training and were a battalion.

Johnny was in third grade, Sara in first, and Nora and Jinny at home. It was at this time that I learned to drink coffee without sugar because of sugar rationing. I bought little sugar bowls and each child was allotted a certain amount. If they used too much on their cereal one or two days, they would have to go without by the end of the week. In early December of 1943, the children came down with sore throats, high temperatures, and ear infections. Dr. Bolan made house calls at that time which was a comfort and a big help to me. I also got the "bug" and ran a high temperature. My mother was staying with us that winter and she was a big help also.

On December 10th, while I had this miserable bug, I received a letter from Van telling me that his battalion was being shipped out in late January (destination unknown, of course) and would it be possible for me to come to Providence RI to visit him for a week early in January 1944? Of course, I would if I had to walk on "hot coals" to get there.

First, we had to get over the flu bug and then Christmas plans had to be made. I had sent an order in to Montgomery Ward in the middle of November for toys, games, dolls, etc., but my check was returned with an "all out" notice, which meant I had to go shopping. Because of gas rationing, I couldn't just hop in the car and take off for Traverse, so I went to Suttons Bay and did quite well.

Along with all of the above, I started on the job of weaning Jinny as I was still nursing her. It was quite a job as she was only six months old and she absolutely rejected the bottle milk. Of course, she was getting cereal and Gerber veggies and fruits. Then I also had to find someone reliable to take over the care of the family, Mother, and house. Dear "Grandma" Kahrs agreed to do it. I don't remember anything momentous or disastrous happening that Christmas, except that the song "White Christmas" came out.

So on January 5, 1944, I was ready to leave, with mixed emotions, as I was so anxious to see my husband but also regretted leaving the kids. There was a 5:00 p.m. train out of Traverse which I planned to take, so I drove in, stored the car at Grand Traverse Auto, and one of the attendants took me to the train station. Train travel was new to me, so it was exciting, but also frightening. I had to change trains in Grand Rapids and again in Jackson. After I boarded the coach at Jackson, I was exhausted. The coach was very crowded but shortly the Pullman conductor came through the coach and he asked me if I would like a berth in the Pullman car as far as Buffalo. It had been reserved but no one showed up. He was a friendly gentleman and told me that he had a cottage at Glen Lake. I was very grateful to him and enjoyed a good rest from 2:00 am until 8:00 am when I had to go back to the coach. I offered to pay for the berth, but was informed there was "no charge."

We arrived in New York Central Station about 5:00 p.m., and I had to find the train gate to New Haven, Connecticut. It was possible to get sandwiches on the NH train, and I was starved. I heard someone say that this train didn't always make connections with the Providence, RI, train, so I checked with the conductor periodically and he assured me it would.

Luella & John K. Van Raalte

We reached Providence about 11:00 pm and Van was there to meet me. How glad I was to see him! He had reservations at the Biltmore Hotel for both of us, but he had to get up at 4:00 am and take a bus to Camp Davis where he was on duty. I slept late, as I was very tired, then hunted up the dining room.

Most of the days I spent exploring the city. The streets were at odd angles and a couple of times I got lost. One day I was able to go to the Base by bus for some function put on for visitors, and Van came back with me. He was able to come into Providence almost every night, and on the weekend we took a bus to Boston. We went to the Harbor to see all of the fishing boats, visited the spot where the Boston Tea Party took place, and went to Child's Restaurant, where we had some excellent seafood, and then had to take the bus back to Providence. One night we went to a restaurant where beautiful organ music was playing. For years after that, whenever I heard organ music, it brought back nostalgic memories and tears.

Postcard from John, Sara & Nora to their parents in R.I.

All too soon, the ten days were up and I had to head for home. I think my bill at the Biltmore was fifty dollars. I don't really remember too much about the train trip home, as my mind was too much on the precious ten days. I did go to Holland and Dad Van Raalte met me at the station and I stayed one night with him and Mother Van Raalte. It was the last time I saw Dad Van Raalte alive. The next day, January the 19th (a Sunday), I took a bus to Traverse City. I forgot that since it was Sunday, I might have a problem getting my car. I did! I called three or more people before I found someone who would get it for me. It was good to get home and see the kids. Mrs. Kahrs had done a marvelous job of taking care of them, and the house was in apple pie order.

A few days later I noted that Sara's cheeks were flushed and her eyes watery. I took her temperature. It was up and I suspected the "real red" measles which I heard were around, so I called Dr. Bolan. He confirmed it and soon red spots did also. Then Nora came down with them, and I had two very sick and uncomfortable little girls with temps over 100 degrees. I remember one very dangerous incident that happened. I kept the room darkened and one evening when I looked, I saw flashes from under the bed. Upon investigation I found a wet washcloth lying on a low cord plugged into the wall. I used washcloths to cool the girls fevered brows, but I was careful not to let that happen again! Dr. Bolan gave Jinny a measles shot, so she didn't get them. John did, but he wasn't nearly as sick as the girls were and had fewer spots. We were quarantined and a "measles" sign put on our front door.

On February 12th, I was awakened at 2:00 in the morning by a phone call from Dora Schurman, Van's sister, telling me that Dad Van Raalte had died. Through the Red Cross, they were able to locate Van. The battalion had already been secured for shipping out, but he was given permission to go home for his father's funeral. He rode day and night on the train to get there. I drove down in the Buick, so this sad occasion brought us together again for a very short time. Floyd, who was also in the Navy and based in Florida, was able to come, and so was Sam, who was in the Army in North Dakota. Albert came also from Traverse City. It was a comfort to Mother Van Raalte to have her four sons with her. Van had to leave immediately after the funeral, so I took him to the train depot in Grand Rapids, where we had another sad farewell.

Then I went on to Belding, as I had Aunt Anna (Mother Van Raalte's sister) with me, and I met her husband Uncle Harry Moor for the first time. Since it was getting late, they insisted that I stay with them instead of driving home as I was alone and it was stormy. I really didn't want to, but realized that it would be the wisest thing to do. They showed me a lot of family pictures, but I wasn't in the mood to enjoy anything. After I went to bed, I cried myself to sleep. The next morning was cold and wintry, but not snowing. I wanted to get underway early, but Aunt Anna wanted me (practically insisted) to drive about ten miles out in the country to see her daughter, Bernice, and children. So I did. Bernice and her husband, Justin, and two boys had been up to see us several times. The drive home was uneventful, but I was exhausted, and so glad to be back home.

Sam Van Raalte, John Van Raalte, Dora Schurman, Nora Keeler Van Raalte, Floyd Van Raalte and Al Van Raalte at home in Holland for the funeral of their father and husband John VanHeuvelen Van Raalte

Editors Note: Luella's notes about the war end here. While Van was in the service, Luella composed the following song "Wishing For Tomorrow" that shows her longing for her husband to be back home.

Wishing for Tomorrow

Luella VanRaalte, 1943

CHAPTER SEVEN

SERVICE IN THE NAVY SEABEES: 1943-45
John K. Van Raalte

Enlisting

I was 36 years old, married, and had four kids when I enlisted. The youngest, Jinny, was three weeks old. I went to Detroit, Michigan, took a Naval examination and was qualified as either a First Class or Petty Officer in the Seabees. I figured I could handle that as I already had automotive school training, had been an automobile mechanic for 12 years, and had run my own establishment for nine of the 12 years. My orders were to report with the next batch of draftees going to Detroit. So when that time came, I went to Detroit and was given the rank of Chief Petty Officer.

We had to hang around Detroit for a couple of days down at an old warehouse on the river. When they got a "draft" together, a guy who was parading around in a uniform informed me that I was to lead the group (about 30 to 50 of us) right down the main street to the railroad depot, and also that I was in charge of the group. He handed me the papers for all of the men.

Chief Petty Officer John K. Van Raalte

Off we went, and when we got to the depot, I was told that I was responsible for getting these guys to Camp Peary, Virginia. As you might surmise, it was darn near impossible to keep track of these guys on a train, but they were pretty well convinced that they had better stay on the train and get off at Camp Peary, so I didn't have any problems. That whole experience was quite an introduction to the Seabees for me.

Training

A bunch of trucks picked us up from the train and away we went. I remember that as we entered the gate to Camp Peary there were a number of Seabees out training with machetes, and as they saw the new bunch coming in, they let out with a big yell, "You'll be sorry!" We were lined up, and the chiefs were separated from the rest of the enlisted men and taken to a detention area. This confinement was for medical purposes, to eliminate anyone with a contagious disease. The area had a 9-foot chain link fence with barbed wire on top. There were barracks in the area and we were told to stay there.

At mealtime, someone came toting a rifle and said "Everybody get out front and form a line of twos," and they marched us off to chow with a rifle! One thing I remember is that we got a mug and were asked if we wanted coffee, tea, milk, or lemonade. For me, coming from the cool upper region of Michigan, I found it hotter than hell at Camp Peary in July. So I said, "Lemonade." Well, the mug was so hot that I could hardly handle it, but they put cold lemonade in it. Of course, we also got beans for breakfast, but I survived.

Chief Petty Officer John K. Van Raalte

We were kept in this detention area for almost a week while they went through an old military routine. We were sent out with shovels to dig. I remember that on the Fourth of July we were out digging a hole, and when we asked what in the hell we were digging it for, the answer was, "So you can fill it back up tomorrow."

Eventually they moved us out of the detention area and gave us a pair of coveralls and an overseas cap and our C.P.O. training began. It was largely done by Marines and they either hated the job or they hated our guts. We sure started out as a sad looking bunch, but the Marines were supposed to make fighting men out of us.

I remember one of the inspections in C.P.O. training. It was an exceptionally hot day but we stood at either "Attention" or "Parade Rest" for two whole hours. The officers rode up in a Jeep, got out and wandered around talking about whatever was on their minds – the liquor they drank the night before, the women they had been out with, the card games they had played – and all the while we were standing. I remember that Bill Henderson, who was standing ahead of me, was sweating so much the sweat was running down his arms and dropping off the ends of his fingers and onto his trousers. Fourteen guys fainted and fell over. The corpsmen came with stretchers, picked them up, and put them in the shade. When we finally were dismissed and marched off the field, we were almost unable to move, our muscles were so stiff. I can still remember how we hated the officers who put us through that ordeal.

Then along came the happy day when they decided we were trained and ready to go. We moved into another area and the chiefs were put into separate quarters with a new bunch of "boots" who had just come in. We were now supposed to train these new men. Except for two chiefs in the outfit who had had military service before, the rest of us didn't know much about military procedure, but we went right ahead.

At our first session, the instructor explained to the welding group that Chief Van Raalte would be in charge. I had purposely eliminated welding from my record, as I had not done much of it. I heard one man say to another, "He'd better be good." And I knew all the men in this group were experienced welders before becoming Seabees. So I got up and said, "I am Chief Van Raalte, and I heard one of you say 'he had better be good.' For your information, I am an automobile mechanic. I know what gas welding is, and I have heard that welding can be done with electricity. Gentlemen, there are three ways of doing something: the right way, the wrong way, and the Navy way. The Navy says I am in charge, so I am. Thank you." They all cooperated very well and I learned how to arc weld.

Two Leaves

We had a 72-hour leave during this period. I was unable to get home in that length of time, so Victor Mark Bogar of Selinsgrove, Pennsylvania, invited me to go home with him. We took the train to Selinsgrove. All of his kinfolks came to see him and they had a great big picnic outside. They were wonderful folks. The trip back to Camp Peary was quite an experience. I remember that the train station in Washington was crowded and everyone was pushing to get on the train. A woman was standing by a steel railing and the crowd pushed so hard that she was pushed against the railing and fainted. Someone had to carry her away. When we got on the train, we had to stand the whole way.

We had another leave before being sent to Providence, RI, and I was able to get home then and see my family. That was the only time during my two years in the service that I did get home. Part of the problem was that I didn't have the money to fly. I had an allotment made out for my wife, Luella, to take care of the family. That was the only income she had. This left me without much spending money and not enough for airfare. A train would always take too long.

Move to Providence/Camp Davis

We were shipped to Camp Davis in Providence, RI, by train. The only thing I remember about it is that we were served a box lunch somewhere along the way.

At Camp Davis, I was assigned to a garage for service work on vehicles. However, the base was run by a "Ship's Service" and there wasn't anything for us guys to do, so we'd go there, spend some time and then return to the barracks. Some military training was thrown in - marching, which no one liked. We invented a lot of ways to beat the game on this.

I do remember that one of the men in my platoon had been out on a detail splitting wood with a wedge and a piece of the wedge broke off and embedded itself in his leg. The head of the Quonset hut asked me to come down and look at the man. He had been sent to sickbay earlier, and a doctor there had said there was nothing wrong with him. By the time I saw him it looked like blood poisoning. He had red streaks running up and down his leg and had a fever. So I went to the Chief and found out there was a second doctor in the battalion. We got the sick man up to this doctor's quarters and I sat there while the doctor dug out the piece of steel, put antiseptic on it, and bandaged it up. The fellow did get better. We were fortunate that the first doctor didn't ship out with us.

Another incident that comes to mind was about our Chief Commissar. He was up most of the night preparing food for the battalion, and so he would sleep during the day. Then in the middle of the night, he would come barging in, sit down, smoke a cigar and sleep for an hour or so before he went back to work. This got to be a pain for the rest of us. We were putting in long days and needed our sleep. So finally three of us in the Quonset decided that we had had enough. One day when he came in to sleep, we picked him up, mattress and all, carried him out, and deposited him in a snow bank. When he woke up, he was damn mad. He grabbed a bolo knife and heaved it at us and the bolo went through the corrugated steel and set there quivering like an arrow. Someone got around behind him, tied him in his bunk and told him there would be no more rough stuff. That wasn't the end, however. About a week later, we were told there was a service club on the base where we could get a beer. The Chief Commissar was there and insisted we go to the mess hall and get a sandwich. In the mess hall, he started cutting the meat for the sandwich, then turned around, grabbed one guy's tie and cut it off with the razor-sharp knife just below the knot at the neck. Then he went back to making the sandwich. Apparently, he felt that he had made his point. We did quit frigging around with him.

Visits and Shipping Out

Luella came to see me at Providence before we shipped out overseas. We went to see a movie that had been made about the "Fighting Seabees."

Just as we were preparing to ship out, the Red Cross got the message to me that my father had died (February 12, 1944). So Commander Redmond gave me permission to go home to Holland for the funeral. Luella was there, and although we were happy to be together again, it also meant the agony of another good-bye. The train ride from Providence to Holland was really rough because there was standing room only. On the way back, it was even worse. I had a seat from Grand Rapids to Kalamazoo, but when I had to change there for the New York Central, it was so crowded that there wasn't even space in the aisles to lie down. Some small guys had climbed up on the racks for suitcases, but I was too big to do that. I finally found a place in the baggage car and went to sleep leaning again the wall. When I woke up, I was all snow and coal soot. At Pittsburgh, the authorities chucked us all off the train, even though it was going straight through to New York. I decided it was all a farce, and got right back on the train, found a seat, and consequently got some sleep before I got back to Providence.

Then came the maneuver of shipping out. We were "secured" with no mail out, no one allowed off the base. All our bedding was taken away, so we had to sleep on the floor with all of our gear ready and clothes on. Then in the middle of the night we were marched to the mess hall to get something to eat. All this so the enemy wouldn't know we were going. But what happens at the last moment? We formed in lines to march to the dock and along came the brass band playing and marching ahead of us all the way. Then we got on board and had to stay below deck so that spies would not be able to report that a shipload of service men were shipping out. As I remember, we laid at dock for a day or more before moving into the Atlantic.

My strongest memory of those days was the taste of the water. The story had it that some dumb yo-yo had filled the fresh water tank with fuel oil, which had to be drained out so the tank could be refilled with water. Anyway, the water tasted like fuel oil. Anything cooked in water, the potatoes and vegetables, tasted of fuel oil. The only things that were really edible were fresh fruits or vegetables or fried meat. Even the coffee tasted like fuel oil.

We ran into a storm off Cape Hatteras, and then in the midst of the storm we were pulled on deck for an "abandon ship" drill. I remember that a submarine was actually sighted in the area. A lot of the guys were sick and threw up all over the deck. It was a mess! My assignment during that storm was to stand watch in the section of the bow of the ship. I had four hours on and eight hours off around the clock. I got really sick myself after looking at all the vomit in the urinal trough. I also remember an officer coming down to the quarters and giving us a lecture on staying with it and being brave. After he left, the guys talked about it and figured that he was scared stiff about the submarine threat.

Going down through the Panama Canal was very interesting. At the exit to the Pacific, we laid in for a day or two while they did some welding on the side of the ship.

Arrival in Honolulu

It turned out that we were being shipped to Hawaii to rebuild the John Rodgers Air Field that had been destroyed in the attack on Pearl Harbor. When we arrived at Honolulu, the ventilating fans in the ship were turned off, and boy-oh-boy was it hot. We all had to remain at the exact place we were assigned to until the ship was unloaded. I remember hours of sitting there wringing wet with sweat before we were allowed to leave ship.

After we were ordered off the ship, we stood out in a compound until some trucks picked us up. We were driven through Honolulu, by Pearl Harbor, then turned off to the right and went up on a hill. We were told that this was our camp.

Even in wartime, the traditional lei welcome to Hawaii

Next I remember we were told that there was a garage setup somewhere below, so we wandered down. We set up a dispatch office in what I remember as a little shack and I was able to get Wilt transferred to transportation as our dispatcher. The drivers and mechanics would turn up there.

Getting the Trucks Rolling

We had a lot of trouble with the junk equipment we were getting at our base to do the construction work. It would take one truck pushing tailgate to tailgate to start another truck. We were trying to figure out where to get some tools, what men knew what, and who could fix what. We also had some trouble with having a new warrant officer in charge of transportation who openly said he didn't know a damn thing about transportation and couldn't care less.

After some time, we did get the repair work rolling so that most of trucks would start on their own each morning. Then I remember Lt. Madison from Headquarters coming over to say that he wanted me to go for a ride with him in his jeep because he had something to show me. He took me over to another big garage setup and said, "Look it over." I said, "Well, obviously somebody is already working here and they have a lot of equipment and vehicles to repair." Then he said, "That's going to be your job. Think you can handle it?"

Van (on left) and unknown Seabee mechanic in Hawaii

I asked how many vehicles we were going to have to keep going, and he said about 175. My reaction was, "You had sure better get me some more mechanics." He told me we'd have about 32 new trucks, but the rest would all be junk. So I went to the dispatch officer and told him to send me five a day that wouldn't start. I said I'd get those trucks back able to start by the next morning and then take another five.

That's exactly what he did. It wasn't too long before it was a rare sight to find one truck pushing another one to start in the morning. This set-up was the biggest operation I handled in the Navy. We had a machine shop, a large welding shop, a heavy equipment shop, and a light equipment shop for jeeps and carry-alls. I'm not sure how many men I mustered, but I had three crews who worked around the clock to keep equipment rolling.

To give you a view of our work, you need to know what our dump trucks did. At that time, the Navy was dredging for coral to use in building an airstrip to connect Hickam Field and John Rodgers Airport so the B-29s would have the space to land. The coral was run from the bottom of the bay through pipes into little lagoons. Then the trucks would back up and be loaded with coral.

We started to have a lot of brake trouble and discovered that a lot of the trucks had corroded brakes. It was one hell of a job pulling those brakes off. With a little investigation, I found one of the company commanders was running trucks that he had down into the salt water right up to the truck bed. So I got Lt. Madison to go over and find out why they were running the trucks into salt water, and if there wasn't another way to do it. He came back and assured me that it would stop.

Van, second from left

Another time, we started to get trucks coming back with the tailgates all bent up like a pretzel. After another investigation, I found out that some wild yahoo was running a crane for loading the coral and he either couldn't hit the truck box or he deliberately hit the tailgate. So I issued an order through the dispatcher that all the trucks should take their tailgates off. The next day, an officer came over ranting about who in the hell had the authority to order the tailgates off. So I said that I did. I told him to look at the stack of tailgates that had to be straightened out and that I figured we could save a few in advance just by taking them off. He said he damn well wanted the tailgates on, but he agreed that he would transfer the wild yahoo on the crane to doing something else.

A Commendation for Work

One of the highlights in my Navy career was when Commander Redmond came to me one day and said, "I know what you're doing, and I like it. If you want anything, or need anything to get this stuff going, and you are unable to get it through normal channels, you have my authority to come direct to me and tell me what it is, and I'll have it to you in two days. I'll send an airplane back to the States and get it. Keep up the good work."

Hell, I puffed up my chest and blew a couple buttons off my shirt at that! I never did actually go to him because we always found what we needed. We had a parts man who knew how to procure, steal, or borrow anything that we needed. If we couldn't find some part, we had an engineering department that was glad to make up a blueprint and send it to the machine shop. Then the boys in the welding department would make it up for us.

As time went on, the word got around the grapevine that if somebody had a piece of truck or equipment that wasn't working, they should bring it on over to the 129th battalion and those boys would fix it. We wound up fixing Army equipment, Marine equipment, and Navy equipment, all in addition to the equipment of the 129th. I started to get a little grief from my guys who were working their fannies off, when they'd see other men sitting around all day without anything to do. They got to hate my guts and then they let me know that, damn it, the rest of these guys should take care of their own equipment.

We had set up a rotation system of getting the vehicles in to change the oil and filter and get the vehicles lubricated on a regular schedule. As dispatcher, Wilt would watch the mileage and send the vehicles in. For the boys on the grease rack, this was damn dirty work and tough because they had to wash their own clothes with a scrub board and a brush. Then we got a lucky break. Somebody from the army came over, needing some equipment we had. And, in return, he said he'd send over some rags, but he sent back two truck loads of army trousers and shirts. Most of the stuff was just like new. From that time on, my grease boys wore army clothes, and when it got too damn greasy; they dropped it in the trash barrel. That really made the grade with those guys.

Pineapple Commandos

Every once in a while, someone in charge would decide it was time for us to have a military maneuver. Then we'd go sit up in the pineapple fields. We called ourselves the Pineapple Commandos. We didn't have any communications apparatus, so we'd usually stop at the top of a hill and get up and wave our hands. Whatever officer had charge of this fiasco would get up and talk about it. If this had been a real war, and Japanese were down below, we'd all have been dead.

Once on a day off, a couple buddies and I were wandering back in the sugar cane and we stumbled onto what happened to be a gun position in the sugar cane field. Suddenly a man stuck a gun in my belly and said, "What are you boys doing up here?" We said, "Hell, we're just walking down through the sugar cane." He said, "You know, if you're smart, you're going to turn right around and go the other way." Obviously, that's what we did.

Our camp was in the hills just below the highest mountains and I remember that back behind us was an enormous barn that was very brightly painted with a red roof and white side walls. One day I was out in my 4-by-4 looking for something to see and I thought I saw this barn move so I stopped. Sure enough, the barn, which was 200 feet by 200 feet, raised itself up in the air and turned around 90 degrees. Then out from under the roof came a gun that probably had a bore of 16 inches. It gave a hell of a boom, and I realized it was a shore battery protecting Pearl Harbor. Then the barn lowered, turned and the gun disappeared. There was just this barn left in a farmyard on the side of a mountain.

The U.S. army had guns hidden in every cave, every cornfield, every cane field, and every pineapple field, all along the beaches. The beaches were one tangled solid mass of barbed wire. Even if a boat had managed to get ashore, men never would have made it up the beach.

One day Henderson and I went down to Pearl Harbor on a procuring job and seeing a submarine tied up, I said to Henderson, "I've never been on a submarine, have you?" And he said, "No, but they're not going to let you either." I said, "How the hell do you know unless we try to find out?" So we went up and saluted the officer of the deck and said, "Sir, we're Seabees. We've never been on a submarine. Could we take a look?" And he said, "Yeah, you could do that. I'll have a guy take you through. But keep your hands in your pockets and don't put them on anything that you see that you don't know what the hell it's all about." What impressed me more than anything was that the torpedoes were stacked along the side, and the sailors on board slept under and on top of these torpedoes. In a submarine there is not one inch of space to spare. It's the most confined thing next to being in a strait jacket in jail. It would have killed me because I hate being confined in small quarters.

Little Annie

One of the interesting experiences in maintenance was that we had inherited two enormous vehicles which had been used at the Panama Canal. Neither one was working, so just out of curiosity, we got one of the engines going. Then we found that the transmission case was busted. So that gave me something to do. I wound up at the army engineers office, which was in Honolulu, and they scrounged around and found me another case, which also turned out to be busted. But I got the army case back to a welding guy who was exceptionally good, and he cleaned the case up, and gas-welded it. Then the rest of the boys got the transmission back together and we got the truck running. Some of the sign boys painted up a sign - we called it Little Annie.

The mechanics of the 129th Battalion in front of "Little Annie"
Van is 5th from the right in the front row

Little Annie was the showpiece of the battalion. It was the biggest equipment on the island and probably the most useless, because it had to be on hardtop or it would go right down in the dirt to the axle. But the 129th battalion got a lot of publicity for getting that equipment going. We also got the second one going and we called it "Little Bertha."

Once Little Annie almost stopped the war effort in the area. Here's how it happened. There was very small bridge outside Honolulu on the way to Pearl Harbor. It was between our barracks and Honolulu. One day, Little Annie had a full load of coral. She swung off the paved surface onto the shoulder and down she went on her outside wheels, at a 45-degree angle, about ready to turn over. Lt. Madison came to me and said I'd better go out and look at it.

So I got Jesse Langwell and the three of us went out and took a look. After a conference, Jesse decided it would take two caterpillars, with two of his best operators, to bring Little Annie upright. The Honolulu police had to be notified so they would stop the traffic and M.P.s had to be notified because of the shore patrol. And the Navy brass had to be notified. We had to start immediately and we were given a limited time to get it finished.

Everything went like clockwork. The first cat got Little Annie upright, and the other cat got her wheels on hard ground. We unhooked the cable and said "Hooray!" Standing all around us were more Honolulu police, shore patrol, and M.P.s than I thought existed on all the islands combined.

Two Tough Guys

I remember that one of the chiefs had a civilian vehicle that he used to run around the island. I knew we didn't have any repair parts for it, and one day I thought I was doing him a favor by telling him that if he broke down and needed a part that wasn't repairable or exchangeable or weldable, he'd be out of transportation. He told me that he would do just as he damned pleased with his vehicle, and if I didn't keep my mouth shut, he'd stick a knife in my ribs.

I looked right back and told him he could do just as he damned pleased, but the fact was that when it quit, there weren't any parts. The other chief told me I never should have said that because he was dangerous. My theory was that he didn't have guts enough to do anything. So I treated him accordingly and went about my business. Once we did happen to come up to a door at the same time and he motioned for me to go out first. I presume that he figured out that when I got mad, I was mean myself, and that he didn't want to tangle with me.

A Day Out

Men of the 129th on a Day Out
Van may be the man in sunglasses seated at front right corner of the table

We were on the Hawaiian Islands for over a year. Our battalion had done such a great job in rebuilding the runway between Hickam and John Rodgers (so the army could set down the B-29s that were bombing Tokyo) that our commander was told give us a day off at the beach with one hell of a lot of food and beer on ice. The boys hadn't had any beer in a long time, so it was a great day.

On the way back to camp, each chief was assigned to a group of men to ensure they got back to quarters. My group was the men who worked in the maintenance garage for me. I had 35 or 40 men in this six by six truck. One guy, a little black-haired fella, was just a little bit higher on the beer than the rest. He saw some Hawaiian women and he decided to jump over the side. So I grabbed him by the belt and hung on - and got kicked in the guts for my trouble.

The rest of the guys, who were playing a game, had started tearing the sleeves off their shirts. Threads rotted in the tropics, so things tore easily. Well, I was hanging on to one guy, and some of the other guys got the idea that since I was more or less helpless, they would have some fun with me.

So some guys threw my cap over, tore my shirt off and threw it over, and then they started on my trousers and ripped a seam clear up to the crotch. They managed to get one leg torn off. When I arrived at camp, I had no cap, no shirt, and only one leg of my trousers on, which flapped in the breeze. Being Chief Petty Officer, I was supposed to maintain a position of dignity among the sailors. Now you try getting off a truck, walking down through the company streets with dignity, when you are practically naked except for shoes. Well, I made it! I got a lot of whistles and catcalls, but I made it.

I got dressed, ate, and got some sleep. The next morning at six I went down to check my crew in. They all played innocent. They just happened to have their heads inside something - under a car, under a hood, under a fender. They just didn't see me. Well, I walked over and said "Good morning. I'm glad you're here in one piece." When it's about 60 to one, you might as well pretend it was a good time. So there never was any hard feeling about the incident, but there was a little kidding about my new clothes. "What the hell happened? Did you lose your old clothes?" That memory sure stuck with me.

Putting A Truck Driver on Report

I remember that one of the truck drivers, about 15 years younger than I was and weighing 80 to a 100 pounds more than I did, had been reported to me for problems. I had examined the trucks and found that he'd broken three axle shafts in a row. So I sent the word out that this guy was to meet me at my office, which was merely a desk sitting in the shop.

I asked him how much he got paid an hour. He said he got two bucks, and I told him he'd been overpaid at a quarter an hour. Well, he proceeded to tell me what he was going to do to me, loudly and in front of about 25 of my men. So I told him that he was younger and weighed more and I was damn sure he could do what he said he was going to do. But I said "I want you to know one thing. I don't have any yellow down my backbone; I didn't get drafted in this outfit; I enlisted. And you don't bother me one damn bit."

I checked the situation out with the chief master-of-arms, who told me to charge him with disrespect. He told me not to repeat what this man said, but to dress in my whites, salute the commanding officer and stand at attention while I listened to him. That's exactly what I did. Then they called in this truck driver, and the result was that he was fined $175 and two weeks in the brig with the Marines. That's tough. In the Marine brig, the guys work digging holes and laying pipes and have to make double-time whenever they move anywhere. During the night, the guards wake them up twice with a bucket of water in the face, after which they have to mop up the cell. And they only get bread and water for food.

After the two weeks, the guy came back looking for me and started out telling me what he was going to do to me. I just said, "You know, if you threaten me again, you go back on report." It never happened. He started to greet me with "Good morning, sir." Seamen did not call chiefs "sir," but that's what he called me. The word got passed to me that he had stopped being trouble.

An Explosion and a Crash

I remember that close to the end of our stay in Hawaii we got an order to clean up our equipment, which meant to sandblast and paint it. We couldn't find a sand blaster, but we found a compressed air machine that was used for pumping concrete into places where you couldn't shovel it in. The trouble was that the coral from the beach that we were going to use as sand was wet. So I remembered a technique that was used in Leland in the winter to dry out gravel to make cement. It involved taking a couple of barrels, cutting the ends out, loading the gravel over the top and building a fire in the barrels to dry out the gravel.

So I had my men set up this process. Everything was going fine until we heard a hell of a big boom. A cloud of black smoke the size of a battleship was going up in the air. Then I heard fire trucks screaming and six of them rushed into the company area. So I headed over to see what was happening. It just so happened that one of my best mechanics, a tall skinny guy from California, had gotten a screwy idea. I'd told him to throw in a couple of buckets of drain oil with the trash wood and paper to get the fire going and then to feed it with wood. But he also threw in five gallons of gasoline, figuring that would help it go faster. It sure whooped the process up!

Since I was in charge, I had to explain to the Honolulu fire department, the Marines, the Army, and the Navy exactly what we were doing and why, without incriminating any of my men. They seemed to think we were trying to blow up Pearl Harbor. From my point of view, it was a very small mistake and didn't hurt anybody.

For recreation at our camp, the mess hall that fed 1,250 men would be set up for movies. One night we had a war movie going that came directly from the army action, and there was a terrific amount of noise in it. Big guns were blowing things up and so on. Right at the climax of the movie, we heard one hell of a big roar and crash, but it wasn't in the movie. What had happened was that one of the truckers had parked his International 6 by 6 dump truck up about 500 feet higher than the mess hall. He'd either left it out of gear or the brakes were off, or both. So it took off by itself and wandered right down to the mess hall. Thankfully, there were two big poles holding some transformers in its way. First it smashed some other trucks, then smashed the poles, smashed the transformers, and stopped the movie right at the climax.

Visit to Sickbay

Once I picked up an allergy from some growth down on the beach where the garage setup was located. The effect was that I'd start sneezing and go on sneezing for four minutes or more. I kept losing sleep at night, until I finally got to the point that I almost could not walk. So I decided I should turn myself into sickbay.

The military has a definite procedure for this. You go down to sickbay and tell them what the ailment is. The doctor looks you over and then says, "You go get your gear and report to sickbay." Go getting your gear means getting your sea bags and possessions from the locker and your bolo machete and semi-automatic rifle. You check it all into a locker at sickbay. Then you are in the doctor's authority until he releases you.

Van in the Philippines

The first thing they did was send in a couple corpsmen to jab me in each hip with an injection that put me to sleep. The next thing I knew, our Lieutenant came barging in and wanted to know what the hell I was doing there. The doctor came down and asked what the hell he wanted. And the Lieutenant said he needed me. Then the doctor told him to get his ass out of there because I was under the doctor's command until he decided I should leave.

That was all right with me because what I needed more than anything was rest. For months I had been trying to get somebody to relieve me on my night shift and I was always told there just wasn't anybody. That meant I had to muster in and muster out three crews of men around the clock. I was down at the garage at six in the morning and at midnight I came down to muster the last crew in.

The doctor knew this. He had stopped me one time in the camp area and said, "When the hell is the Lieutenant going to get you some relief? He's working you to death." And I said, "Well, I've been trying, but he says he can't get me any relief." And the doctor said, "That's a crock. I can point out 100 men that haven't done one damn thing for six months."

Finally, the doctor decided I was all right, so I was ordered out, and I picked up my gear and bolo machete and appeared back on the job. This experience was unique for me.

A View of the War

Because of the location of the garage right on the bay I could see the ships come in from the war zone bombed all to hell and with holes in them. I remember one of the aircraft carriers up in dry dock for repair with holes all over it. I saw hospital ships come in and unloading and the planes bringing in wounded. We knew when one was coming because the military ambulances would all converge waiting for the plane's arrival. The living were put on stretchers and run like hell to the hospitals, and the dead were put to the side. Somebody went by with buckets of water to mop up the blood and get ready for the next load.

One morning a B-29 tried to take off three times and they kept having to abort the take-off and go back and fix something. Well, the last time, the pilot got off the runway and then set her down on a road about 15 feet above the level of the runway. I happened to be right in position to see it land and I saw the airmen drop out of it. These fellows were opening the doors and dropping and running as fast as they could get from it. That B-29 had a full load of bombs for Tokyo and was full of gasoline for the run and could have exploded.

I remember that the Marines came in, put a guard around it, and then, after a waiting time, started to investigate. We sure were glad to see it go because when it came down I was close enough that I made a dive on my belly (and so did everybody else) on the back side of the Quonset on the ground and was hoping that I was safe.

Van in front of Quonset Hut

There were a lot of military maneuvers going on and a lot of them didn't go according to plan. I had seen too many airplanes hit each other in the air in a ball of fire and then the parts came floating down. We all knew that the parents back in the U.S. would get a letter about how their son had died valiantly fighting the enemy. Occasionally we'd see a parachute coming down and we'd holler, "Hooray, I guess he made it."

One kind of dive-bombing plane had a four-bladed propeller and was about the most powerful one built then. I remember that there was a rock jutting out in the ocean on the far side of the island from the city of Honolulu and that occasionally I'd go over there to get material from the civilian airport for the battalion and see these planes in practice. These fellows would dive for the rock and let their bomb go, with the idea of hitting the rock each time.

We always knew when the Marines were going out on another invasion because for their military maneuvers, they usually carried just one canteen. But on the day they were going on ship they had full military gear and two canteens.

I remember that the 133rd battalion was supposed to relieve us but the big brass decided they wanted to keep us on so instead, they shipped them out. The word soon got back to us that the men in the 133rd had been all shot up. Many years later, when Luella and I were on the way from Texas to Oregon, we stopped at Port Hueneme, Los Angeles, where the Seabees have a museum. They had a little chapel and a very big bronze plaque with the names of Seabees that were killed in WWII. We took the time to look up the 133rd. What had been merely rumored during the war was indeed fact. The only reason it wasn't us was that we were experienced and got to stay in Honolulu.

Another fact that comes to mind is that the Seabee battalion was segregated. The only colored people in the battalion were servants of the officers. Believe it or not, each officer had a servant who put his meal in front of him and took his dirty plates, took his laundry, made up his bed and swept out his quarters. This in a war in which GIs are lying in holes and caves, sleeping on decks. I saw thousands of wounded men in the Philippines laying on a platform in a cot with a screen around it to keep malaria and mosquitoes away, and that was it. But the officers were a different breed of people.

I remember the one time that F.D.R. (President Roosevelt) came to visit the Hawaiians. The total military put on one of the biggest shows of the war for his benefit. Everything that could fly, roll on wheels, or float was in performance. And every inch of road that he traveled in his motorcade was lined with shore patrol MPs and Honolulu police. His motorcade went right by the garage that I was in charge of because it was on the main road from the airport. We had spent the two days prior to his arrival fixing up the place. We actually polished it, even though he never came any closer than the road. Anyway, as he went by, the boys of the 129th all lined up, and I remember with pride my Seabees yelling out "Hi ya Frankie! How are ya?"

Thoughts on the Bombing of Pearl Harbor

If you get a map of Honolulu and look at it closely, you'll realize that Pearl Harbor is a natural harbor whose entrance is a very, very small neck of water. It seemed to us that the ships that were sitting in Pearl Harbor in 1941 had all been docked side by side, like checkers on a checkerboard. All the Japanese had to do was fly down, let the bombs loose, and they were going to hit something.

While I was in Hawaii, I had the opportunity of talking maybe five or six times to Professor Barrett, who had taken an exchange professorship at the University of Honolulu and was there when the Japanese came in on attack in December, 1941. He happened to be sitting on his porch up on the mountainside that morning and saw the whole show. Evidently, the big mistake the Japanese made was that they didn't follow up their air attack. If they had, they would have gotten the Hawaiian Islands, and we would have had to fight the Japanese from the U.S. West Coast.

One of the views I held was that Roosevelt and the Administration knew the Japanese were advancing. They had gone down through China, taken Hong Kong, taken the other islands, the Philippines, and so on. The military had even practiced a maneuver for what to do if the Japanese did try a sneak attack on our ships in Pearl Harbor. A lot of us felt it wasn't that the officers were so stupid as to let it happen, but that Roosevelt and the really big brass knew that we were going to have to fight the

Japanese, but that they had to get public opinion behind the decision to go to war.

So in my opinion they actually set up a psychological situation that they knew would make the American public so mad at the Japanese that we were willing to fight, which is exactly what happened. We went to war on two fronts at once and won on both of them. It wasn't because our military was that damn good, but because we had a civilian population willing to produce the ships, guns, shells, and other armament faster and better than ever had been done in the world before.

A View of Hawaii

The men in our battalion were well aware that Honolulu was one of the world's richest cities and it catered to the ultra-rich from the East, from India, China, Japan, Burma. These people were not just millionaires they were billionaires. I remember picking up the Honolulu newspaper at a time when you could buy a very good watch in the U.S. for $50 and reading Honolulu advertisements for watches that cost $1,000 or $5,000. You don't advertise that sort of thing unless you expect to sell some.

Wandering down the streets of Honolulu, we Seabees felt a little like the country boy who hasn't cleaned all the manure off his shoes or brushed all the hayseed off his shirt. It felt as though we should apologize for entering a shop.

The two big exports from Hawaii were sugar and pineapples. We saw all the tropical fruits: bananas, oranges, lemons, papayas, and grapefruit. I saw my first banana tree in Honolulu, and I remember being utterly amazed that the bananas pointed upward as they grew on the trees and not down, as they would hang in a fruit store. Trucks would come into town from the pineapple plantations and a guy with a loudspeaker would announce, "There's work in the pineapple fields today." Once they picked up enough local men, they would truck them back to the fields for the day.

Because of our excellent work at the airport, the Air Force decided to take the men of the 129th over from Oahu to the big island of Hawaii for a two or three day vacation. It was a marvelous experience. I saw the volcano, the sulfur boiling out of the ground, and the molten rock boiling. The big island had a lot of cattle.

I remember that they had a little narrow train that was used to haul sugarcane around the island, and that it also hauled passengers. The locomotive actually was a U.S.-made little white truck. All of the cars were open flat cars with benches. We saw just fantastic scenery up in the mountains. At one place we saw how they tapped the water supply, built flumes on stilts; then they put the sugar cane in the flumes so it would shoot on the water down to the factory at the beach. So the cane would go roaring down those flumes from about 4,000 feet up in the mountains, sometimes across valleys that were 500-600 feet deep.

One unique memory is of the little train engine stopping where there was a little creek running along by track. And I saw that some ingenious person had made a paddlewheel and then had a fruit jar of cream attached to the paddlewheel, so that as the water ran over the paddlewheel, the fruit jar would turn end to end and make butter. I thought this was very smart.

Back to the States - and on to the Philippines

Suddenly I got an order that I was to get secured to go back to the States. I asked why, and everybody said "We don't know. But you secure your baggage and report to the air strip at such and such an hour." Well, through scuttlebutt, I discovered that four chiefs were going. None of us knew why, but we guessed that some equipment was going to be shipped to our next assignment, which turned out to be the Philippines, and that we were supposed to oversee this. The idea was to be sure that some other battalions didn't latch on to the equipment before we got to our destination.

So we flew back to the States. Well, it certainly was a big joke. When I got on to the ship that I was assigned to and headed back into the Pacific, the only thing on the ship was pontoons for making pontoon docks and piling for making more docks. What this automobile mechanic was doing on a ship with pontoons and pilings, I never knew.

We shipped out to the Philippines. I was on board that ship for 55 days with absolutely no duty. But before I had left Honolulu, I had gotten myself a little set of Exacto carving knives and some native Koa wood that is a cross between mahogany and walnut. My intention was to carve something out of this. And on the ship I sure needed some way to kill the boredom. So I sat on deck while the Pacific lived up to its name - there wasn't a wind that blew during the whole 55 days.

Anyway, I sat on the deck and carved the initials for our daughter Sara. I carved "Sara Sue." The blocks were about two inches square and about 1/2 inch thick. I cut every bit of the letters with a knife, and then I polished them, sanded them, and went down to the engine room and got some engine oil to oil them. Then I used toothpaste and a toothbrush to polish them. I always thought they were absolutely beautiful, and day after day and hour after hour I'd sit there whittling and carving these letter blocks.

The other thing I remember from that trip was that all exits from inside the ship were triple sealed so that at no time at night would light project out of the ship for a submarine to see and be able to take a crack at you. That also means you have no ventilation, and when you're only five degrees from the Equator, it gets hot. It was so hot that sweat would puddle on the sheets.

A bunch of us decided that we'd try to sleep on deck. That was fine until we discovered that we also had enormous rats on board, about 12 inches long, that weren't a bit scared of us. One came about six inches from my head one night and I decided after that that I could take the heat a lot easier than a rat bite, which might kill you on board ship.

I also remember that we had an unidentified plane come zooming around, so that we had to get on deck with our lifejackets and M-1 rifles and be prepared to abandon ship, hoping that if the ship went down that we'd go down damn fast also. Anyway, it turned out that this was the passage from the Johnson Islands, which had an Air Force base. The pilots were bored because they were too damn far from the war, so just for the hell of it, they'd fly down and zoom over the ship to make their life a little more interesting. It sure made our life more interesting.

Editor's Note: Van's taped recordings about the war end here. Van served on Samar in the Philippines until the war ended.

CHAPTER EIGHT

STORIES ABOUT THE KIDS

Luella M. Van Raalte

<u>1936</u>: We had moved from the Old Dalton House to the Will Stander house, which was just south of Stander Marine. It was luxurious! It had a basement, a bathtub and running water!

Van decided that he would like to make some wine, so he got a small keg of wine started and put it near the fireplace. Johnny, who was 1-½ or 2 years of age at that time, decided to stick the stove grate shaker into the jug of wine that had been left open. No one saw him do it. Van looked for the shaker all over the house and couldn't find it. Several weeks or months later

John D. (Johnny) Van Raalte

when the wine jog was emptied into another container, there was the shaker! We knew that Johnny had dropped it in because he loved to do that sort of thing.

Needless to say, the wine was extra strong that year, and very good! In later years Van put a tight cap on the wine jug.

1938: When Johnny was about four years old and we were living in the big house on Main Street, he and Viola Anderson's daughter of about the same age were playing on the Lindquist dock and Johnny fell in the river! The water was deep and he couldn't get out. The little girl screamed and fortunately her mother was out in the garden and heard her, came running and saved Johnny's life by pulling him out. Van and I were so grateful we didn't know how we could ever repay her, but we did take her and her husband out to dinner to show our gratitude.

Johnny, John and Tom Lindquist & Sara

1940: Being a boy, Johnny had to climb trees, but the tree he chose one time was a tricky one and he fell. He broke his collarbone and the doctor put a leather strap contraption on it to hold it in place while it healed. He kept complaining that his shoulder was so itchy. Turned out that he had fallen into poison ivy and had a rash under leather strap. No wonder it was itchy!

1942: I was reading a Sunday school lesson to Sara today. It was the story of Moses reminding the people how good God had been to them - giving them food, water and shelter. I then asked Sara what food God had given the Israelites in the desert and she promptly replied, "Vitamins, vegetables and fruit." At least she has learned her dietetics.

1943: It was a bright frosty night and the sky was filled with stars that twinkled and looked so close. The children were watching them when suddenly Nora Lynn (3 years old) rushed out to the kitchen all excited and exclaimed, her eyes shining, "Mommy, could we go out and get a handful of stars to sprinkle on the cookies? I'm sure Daddy could get some if he stood on the kitchen stool!" Bless her little heart.

Johnny, Luella & Sara on front porch of 411.S. Main St. house

One Sunday the children and I went to church leaving Van at home alone. When we returned the children immediately wanted to know what he had done while we were gone and Van said,

"Why I prowled all over, up in the attic, down in the cellar and everywhere looking for 'wiffinpoofs' but nary a 'whiffinpoof' could I find." A few weeks later Van was home alone again and when we returned Nora Lynn said, "Did you find a 'whiffinpoof' today?" Van answered "Yes!" and led us upstairs. There on the floor was a bunch of rock wool insulation that he had pulled out of one of the partitions, so ever since rock wool has been 'whiffinpoofs' to Nora Lynn.

As a last adventure before Van and Bud Anderson left for the war Johnny, Van and Bud Anderson hiked out at Pyramid Point. They took a can or two of pork and beans so that they would have something to eat. Van said "I know how to cook them, you bury the can in the sand and build a fire over it" which they did but the can exploded and there were beans and fire all over! They ate what they could salvage and Van and John camped out for the night. Bud had gotten a bad sunburn and decided to walk to the road and hitch a ride home.

1948: Jinny (4 years old) came rushing in the house and excitingly exclaimed, "Mommy, there is a whole row of 'spare ribs' in the garden!!" I repeated, "Spare ribs?" and she said, "Yes." Then I realized that she meant "rhubarb." Funny little monkey!

Jinny, Nora, Sara, Johnny and Van

Sara and Nora are in Holland visiting Grandma Van Raalte - and I remarked, "I wonder if the girls are getting homesick." Jinny looked at me in a surprised way and said, "You mean 'away sick', don't you?"

The other day Sara said, "When I grow up and get married, I hope I won't have a child like me. I'd lose my patience."

Went to the County Fair; Johnny, Dickie Carlson, Sara, Nora, Aunt Agnes and Edward Hahnenberg. It was fun watching the children. They enjoyed it so much.

The whole family went swimming at Bubbling Springs and we all enjoyed it, but someone has to be on guard at all times, and keep counting heads.

Dorothy and Peter LaCamera are here for the weekend. Dorothy brought over some liquid bacon fat in a small can and set it on the kitchen table. I was talking to her and when I turned around Karen was very happily pouring the fat over her shoes. She was sitting on the floor and making a puddle of it. What a mess!

Dorothy and Peter LaCamera with Nora heading out for a hike

Today I received a letter from my niece Genevieve. I had to comb Jinny's and Sara's hair for school and so I put the letter down until later. After the children had gone to school I went to pick up the letter and couldn't find it anywhere. I looked everywhere, under the cedar chest, the tables, and couch, but couldn't find it. I thought Sara must have gathered it up with her geography book and taken it to school. In the afternoon I looked in the little coal heater (there was no fire in it) and there was my letter! Chucked in by Karen. She likes to put waste paper in the stove or coal basket. Sara didn't appreciate it at all, since I made her make an extra trip up to school to look for it.

Johnny is working on an old typewriter someone gave him, and is getting it in working order although the party that gave it to him said it was rusted beyond repair.

Johnny, Karen and I went to Traverse today to have Johnny's glasses adjusted and get him some shoes. We had some deluxe hamburgers from the J&S and Johnny bought some doughnuts. Did we ever enjoy them.

Have been busy canning peaches and tomatoes all week. Sara and Nora slept in the Soper's tent last night. They liked it. Johnny slept in it Wednesday night. This morning Sara spilled a little hot oatmeal on Nora's finger while dishing it up. Nora said it hurt so I put butesin picrate ointment on it and started bandaging it up, when suddenly Nora said, "Oh-oh, mommy, I'm going to faint." And, plop, down she went on the floor. We carried her in on the couch and put cold cloths on her head. She came to in a few seconds but I kept her home from school because she felt woozy. I went to a kitchen shower for my niece Marilyn in the evening.

Sara, Jinny and Nora with Karen in baby buggy

Today is Nora's birthday, and she keeps reminding everyone of the fact lest we forget. She likes her presents very much. She and Sara are going to Patricia Lund's birthday party this afternoon.

Van, Karen and I went to Traverse today. I bought a dress. It is black with birds outlined in blue on it; also I bought a pair of earrings to go with it. Yum, yum, I like it! At home, Jinny and Nora got their own lunch. Jinny ate 3 wieners and a piece of cake.

Have been busy canning. Karen is such a little helper. I was in the bathroom and she was busy in the kitchen. When I came out she had about ten breakable plates and saucers stacked on top of a sugar bowl. She is an expert stacker upper.

1949: Sara and Janie Paupore put on a circus this afternoon. They had crepe paper, balloons, Kool-Aid and cookies. Lots of acts and lots of fun. It was a success. Nora went over to Uncle Fred and Aunt Agnes's to stay overnight.

It was 9:15 p.m. and we were eating black raspberries when suddenly we could hear a dim whir-r-r-ing sound (an outboard motor in the distance). Jinny, who is six, said, "Sara, the night-crawlers are out tonight. I just heard one."

Potato digging vacation from school, but the girls and I dug dirt out of the house instead of digging potatoes. We had the downstairs clothes closet cleaned out, ready to put the "junk" back in. While it was drying and airing out, I stopped to get dinner. Later we went back to work - and what did we find? Karen (2-1/2 years old) blissfully making sand pies in our clean clothes closet! Did I scold her? No. It was such a lovely playhouse, so I let her finish her pie.

1951: One day I was singing, "Somebody loves you, wants to be near you wherever you go." Karen, aged 4, said, "I know who, Mommy. Your guardian angel does!"

1953: Karen and I were watching two woodpeckers pecking away in a tree outside the dining room. Later, Van came home with Lyle

Eitzen's truck. It was high and knocked a limb off the tree in which the woodpeckers had been. Shortly after that Karen called me, "Mommy, Mommy. Come here and see what those woodpeckers did. They pecked a limb right off the tree!" Well, did we laugh? You guessed it, we sure did. Funny little pumpkin.

<u>1954</u>: Rosie (2-1/2) had finished her triple immunization shot at Dr. Bolan's. She was very good and when she got home she excitedly told everyone, "The Doc-or gave me a hot, two huckers and a handy bar."

October 1952 Front: Sara, Jinny, Karen, Rosie, Nora and John with Van and Luella standing. (Luella's dress is the one she mentions buying in 1948)

Rosie was working her State puzzle. The pieces had expanded and would not fit together, so, Rosie said, "Dammit! I can't work it. Dammit!!" Well! I was surprised to say the least and wondered where on earth she had picked that up, so I said, "Rosie, that is not a nice word to use. Who did you hear using it?" Rosie looked at me and calmly said "Cin-nerella." "Cin-nerella" is an imaginary playmate to whom Rosie talks on the phone, etc. Well, I was stymied, and I sure didn't find out from whom she picked it up!

Karen, Nora, Rosie & Luella

<u>1961</u>: Van talking to me said, "The Enterprise staff is going..." he paused and looked at a picture in the magazine he was reading. Rosie (10 years old), all ears, decided to finish the sentence for him, so she added "to pot." What he was going to say was "to Manistique this week-end to see the paper mills." It irks her to have people leave unfinished sentences suspended in air, and she loves to finish them with her own ideas. Another example: We were talking today at the table about the shortcuts in cooking such as pre-cooked rice. Karen said, "The younger generation of today depends..." and she left it suspended, so Rosie quickly added, "entirely too much on the older generation!" It behooves one to finish one's own sentences with one's own thoughts. Karen was going to say, "on commercially prepared foods."

CHAPTER NINE

Halloween 1960 – A Dramatic Rendition
Luella M. Van Raalte

<u>1960</u>: As usual, Halloween was hectic at our house. In the few hours between the end of the school day and bedtime the following took place:

Rosie: Mother, did you call Martha's mother to see if she can stay overnight?
Luella: No, dear, I didn't. I thought that it was all arranged.
Rosie: (In an exasperated tone.) Of course not! You have to call or she can't come.
Luella: All right, all right, I'll call shortly.
Rosie: Oh, and are you going over to pick up Mary for the party? (Mary lives about four miles away and the party is at a home in Leland.)
Luella: (Slightly bewildered.) Was I supposed to?
Rosie: Yes. You said that you would if she didn't have a way.
Luella: Oh. (Sigh) All right, I will.

Phone rings

Luella:	No, Karen isn't here. She is working at the shop tonight. Will you please call later?"

Luella starts dinner and phone rings again. She answers.

Caller:	This is Mary's mother. I don't quite remember what we said about the party. Mary says that you are coming to pick her up at 6:30. Is that right?
Luella:	Well, I really didn't know just what was happening. Rosie just now said that Mary couldn't come until 7:30 and would I go and get her, which I will be glad to do.
Mary's Mom:	Pete could bring her over but he has to take the boys to the party at Lake Leelanau and that won't be over until 7:30, and he could bring her over after that.
Luella:	I have to take Jinny to the dance at Lake Leelanau at 7:30 so I might as well stop in for Mary and save you a trip.

Mary's Mom agrees, and Luella goes back to preparing dinner but Rosie has been listening.

Rosie:	I had better call Ticia and tell her we will be late. The party is supposed to start at 7:00." She calls Ticia.
Rosie:	Mary and I will have to be about a half hour late because Mama has to take Jinny over to Lake Leelanau and she doesn't want to make two trips and Jinny doesn't want to go until 7:30.
Ticia:	But Rosie, what will we do until you come? We don't want to play games or go out and trick-or-treat until you get here. Can't you come any earlier?
Rosie:	Just a minute, I'll talk to Mama. Mama, Ticia is upset because we're going to be late, can't you do

something about it? Maybe you had better talk to her mother."

Luella, trying to get dinner into the oven, comes to the phone.

Luella:	Our daughters certainly seem to be having trouble. But it is like this - I have to take Jinny to Lake Leelanau at 7:30 and I certainly don't want to make two trips so I'll pick up Mary on the way home. They will only be a half hour late.
Ticia's Mom:	That's perfectly all right. A tempest in a teapot, it sounds like.

Jinny comes downstairs and hears the end of the conversation.

Jinny:	Mother, do you want me to take Karen to the party at 6:30?
Luella:	Is Karen going to the party at Lake Leelanau?? She told me the other day that she didn't want to go, but if you take her over you could pick Mary up on your way back and she and Rosie wouldn't have to be late for the party!
Van:	(*sitting in the living room waiting for dinner*) "Oh boy, am I glad I don't have to be in on this!

Luella goes back to getting dinner. Luella then remembers she hasn't called Martha's Mom to see if Martha can stay overnight so she does, but no one answers. Dinner finally gets prepared and everyone sits down to eat. The phone rings and it is for Karen. Luella remembers that she didn't call Mary's Mom to tell them that Jinny would pick Mary up at 6:45 instead of 7:30 so she does that as soon as she is finished eating. Karen goes to get ready, Rosie clears the table, Van goes back to the shop. Jinny reads the paper and Luella made the above-mentioned phone call. Rosie got her costume on and at 6:20, Jinny, Karen and Rosie left for L.L. Luella again called Martha's Mom and found out that Martha couldn't stay overnight. The doorbell rings and the first "trick-or-treaters" arrived. Luella had thought that she would get the dishes done before the "doorbell siege" started, but didn't make it. Phone rings.

Caller: "Is Jinny there?"
Luella: "No, I'll have her call you when she gets home."

Van returned at 7:00 and he decided that he would rather take Jinny to the dance than stay and answer the door bell. Our neighbors brought their candy over for us to give out for them because they had to attend a meeting. We gave out the three packages that we bought, plus two dozen homemade sweet rolls, plus a double batch of fudge.

Van returned from taking Jinny to the dance and Karen returned with him, plus her friends Belinda and Gladys. Karen nonchalantly informed Luella that they were going trick-or-treating and then the girls would need a ride home. Luella vaguely remembered having promised to see that they got home if they came over. Whew, what a day!

CHAPTER TEN

LETTERS FROM LUELLA: 1955-56

Luella M. Van Raalte

These are excerpts from letters that Luella wrote to daughter Sara while Sara was at college.

Last week's Enterprise had a front page item on the unusual jury case settled by a jury of 11 men and 1 woman. I was that woman! I enjoyed the ride in the sand dune car that was part of the trial and the beautiful views but the case itself was a dry one and very easy to decide.

Rosie wrote you two letters and gave Daddy strict orders to mail them. He didn't the first time and she really bawled him out, so he put them in his pocket, and a week later she asked him if he had mailed them. He said "yes" and then asked her who they were to. She said "Sara." So, when you write, you might mention receiving them, even though you haven't. Rosie has a very definite mind.

I'm listening to the squeaks and squawks and occasional melody of Jinny practicing on her clarinet. Pupils from St. Mary's can take band lessons now and Jinny was so thrilled and wanted to so badly. She had her first lesson today and already she can play a whole octave.

Luella, circa 1960

John said [while on leave from the Navy] that there is no place like home. As for me, I'm trying to clean house and am wracking my brains for a substitute for Rosie using the front porch for a playhouse. She has so much fun out there, but it looks like the dickens. Actually, I feel it is much more important for her to have a place to play than it is to keep the porch looking spick and span.

Van went to second Mass this morning and then came home and started pacing around and chewing on a cigar. It developed that all of the unfinished billing at the shop was getting him down, but I had planned to spend as much time today as he wanted to help get them straightened out. We worked from 12:00 to 4:30 at the shop, and then came home to a dinner Nora cooked: nice round steak with gravy, mashed potatoes, vegetable, and "walnut kisses" for dessert. We were hungry and really appreciated it.

Karen and Rosie went to bed, but Karen just came down a few minutes ago to say she was worried about what would happen at the end of the world. Practically, I worry more about the fact that occasionally she feels faint in church. Last Sunday she walked out of church, and I was mentally biting my fingernails about what was happening. She said later that she wasn't faint, but she felt as if she might possibly start feeling faint. And then she got all absorbed watching a black cat outside and never came back.

Karen, Rosie, Nora & Jinny
with Marc Gallini peaking into the picture (on left)

Well. I can come up for air now. Wrote out a thousand dollars' worth of checks today, made out two bank deposits, made out Consumers Power report, figured out the Western Union, Michigan Bell, and Consumers Power accounts for the month, wrote a couple shop letters, finished the daily record sheet, and made up a couple bills. Meanwhile in the background, the back and front doors opened and shut, and I answered questions: "Can I go for a ride with Betty?" "Can Sandy have supper here?" "What's there to eat?" "Do you have the scotch tape?" Got wood in the stove and answered the phone. It's a quiet life!

Nora is in charge of doing dishes but Jinny and Karen are supposed to help. Tonight, Nora was being diplomatic instead of battening Jinny's and Karen's ears down. They had started arguing about who had to dry the first sink full, and Nora said "The one who dries first gets the smallest sink full." So Karen dashed out to start. Jinny is practicing her music on the clarinet and doesn't want to leave it.

Jinny at side of home at 411 S. Main St.

On her kindergarten report letter, Mrs. Eitzen stated that Rosie liked to sing songs alone, and I wish you could hear her sing! Last week Mrs. Eitzen made vegetable soup for the class. She took the group out to her farm to get the vegetables, and then went to the store for the meat, and then they helped prepare the vegetables, all of which Rosie enjoyed. But she doesn't like vegetable soup and so she worried and worried about how she would get out of eating it. The whole process took several days, so when the day arrived, Mrs. Eitzen said if they didn't like the soup after tasting it, they didn't have to eat it; so she went, she tasted, and she ate most of it. Rosie said they saw cows at the farm but it didn't smell very good.

Nora got an A-plus in English and a favorable comment from Sister Armand. Nora was pleased and coupled with the fact that she is learning to drive, she is much happier. She started in on cleaning this week and really went to town. She sang over and over again "Love and Marriage, Love and Marriage, they go together like a horse and carriage."

Sister Thomas Aquinas asked Nora to make a Valentine cake for the Sisters and she made a beautiful one. Tomorrow she has Emily's wedding cake to bake. She has to stay home to do it and it would happen to be the day the supervisor is visiting St. Mary's. Sr. Armand called to say that Nora was one of the students who could recite well in class and could she please come to school. They agreed that if Nora came to 9:35 sociology class, she could then go home and bake the cake. Sr. Armand was pleased that she came, and Nora was happy, even though our oven unit burned out and she had to bake five layers at Mary Nedow's. The cake was a big one and very beautiful.

Rosie with cake made by big sister Nora

Jinny is making a skirt for Nora from a really heavy wool material. It is really a coat material, but she is doing a great job. Nora wants it for the dance tomorrow night, but I'm sure that Jinny will get it done. She doesn't get fussed or hurried but works right along. Of course, she has to practice her clarinet lessons, and last night she had 4H after school.

Karen will play on TV at 5:30 this Saturday. Mrs. Finn's music class has a half hour and Karen is playing "The Snake Dance" for 15 seconds.

I must tell you about the fire that occurred Wednesday night. The fire phone rang at 1:30 am and it was the Traverse operator reporting a fire at the Walter Egeler farm; so I got my first chance to blow the siren; also called Dino Ziebell, and then stayed on the phone to inform any firemen who asked where the fire was. Cliff Egeler called and got to the station to drive the truck. Jackson took the tanker and Van rode with Dino in the Rescue Unit. When they got to the Egeler farm, the basement was full of smoke. So Van put on a Scott air-pack and went in with a hose and a light and a rope attached to him. He couldn't see much of anything but found the fire and he doused it. The basement was full of rubble, piled lumber, potato crates, baby buggies, trikes, and what-not. Once he stepped on a bedspring. Then suddenly the air on the air-pack gave out. He said it felt as if someone had clamped a hand over his nose and mouth. He got out, got another cylinder of air and went back in. It was a successful operation for Leland, not only because the fire was stopped, but everything went like clockwork - protocols, equipment, and portable pumps. The fire was re-fought all the next day, verbally.

Rosie got your letter and was so proud of it; she had to show it to everyone. She says she will make you an extra mud pie when you come home, if the weather is right, of course.

Nora may have written you that her party was a success. I'm glad because it was her first one and important. About 25 kids came, and that was plenty, especially when they started playing a game that required stomping with their feet. Van had gone to bed and when they started that, he came into Jinny's room upstairs, where I was, and said "Are they going to keep THAT up all night???" Actually he was right. They did for quite a while. So he switched bedrooms. The party was over at 12:30 and everyone reported having a good time.

A letter from John states that he received his orders to go to PARIS! Lucky guy, says Nora. He will have a 30-day leave in April before leaving. Van and Nora (the connivers) have planned to drive him to New York and then bring his car (the Studebaker) back here, and Nora plans to persuade John to let her drive it. It's worth a try!

Nora called me a 'doll' last night. She had missed the school bus because she was decorating the hall for Mardi Gras. She had borrowed a skirt from Esther Cordes and still had the hem to turn up. I knew her time would be limited, so I did it yesterday morning. She came rushing in, lamenting the fact that she still had to do the hem of the skirt, then came rushing down to express her appreciation. She and Joanie went with Bonek and Gordie, who dressed in Van's blue uniforms as Navy men. The dance was a success.

Jinny is having a party here tonight, or rather; her class is, as it is a cooperative affair. Jinny furnished the house, pop, and cake. The others furnished hot dogs, buns, and potato chips. They have enough to feed fifty kids, and there are seventeen. They're out on a scavenger hunt now and then will dance. There was only one small bag of potato chips left; these kids must have been empty to their toes.

Nora is wandering around like a lost soul tonight. She made arrangements with Luella Couturier to go to a show, but Van drove off in the Chevy not knowing of her plans, and we can't find him anywhere. She biked all over town looking. We finally saw Van driving down back street; Nora found him and now has the Chevy, so she is happy.

We have been discussing house finances the past few weeks, and it appears that I don't always spend wisely, but I do spend. The subject of Van handling the money has been discussed, and today Rosie chimed in with "Dad is going to take over the finances on Friday." I said, "Well, at least our money problems are no secret." And Rosie said, "No they aren't. I've already told several other kindergarten children about the whole thing."

Remember the St. Christopher statue for the car that Luella Couturier gave Nora to guarantee safe driving? Well, he stays on the dashboard for Nora, but almost every time I get in the car, he falls down and rolls under the seat. Van says that if even St. Christopher won't ride with me, it's time to stop driving. One day both the St. Christopher medal and the statue fell down.

The temperature here is 14 above zero and it is still snowing and blowing here. No school today anywhere in Leelanau County. Jinny is out sleigh riding and has been since 11 a.m., with Betty Lou. I called a few minutes ago to check at Betty Lou's, thinking they would be getting cold. They came home, ate over there, and are playing monopoly.

I took Karen to Traverse to have her eyes checked. I wanted to get her a corduroy jumper, but we ended with the cutest blue corduroy skirt and jacket. The minute she saw it, she fell in love with it and would have nothing else. She also wanted new frames for her glasses, but that will have to wait until her head grows!

Van told Nora this noon that he would pay her if she would get my ironing caught up. She agreed to, but right now is out ice-skating, without pay, with Jinny and Betty Lou. I didn't have the heart to insist on her ironing today since the skating is good and tomorrow snow is predicted.

Rosie isn't as much interested in her Christmas presents as she is in wrapping up things in the leftover paper and string and giving presents to everyone. Next to that comes the fun of dressing up in old clothes. So lots of string and paper and old clothes are all over the living room. I don't know if I'm training her right or not.

John came home last night at midnight, driving 60 hours straight from California. He picked up two hitch-hikers, GIs, who came most of the way. Last night, I just couldn't sleep, and listened to every car, so I heard him when he drove in, although we didn't expect him for several more days. He nearly froze, having just a light jacket, no boots, and his heater quit in Illinois somewhere. It was 14 deg. above zero when he rolled in. We had to play musical rooms. John slept in his old room; Jinny went into Sara's old room; and Karen ended up with Rosie.

Rosie playing "dress-up" at 411 S. Main house

Rosie, John D. & Karen

Rosie gets such a kick out of Van and John's "'shop talk." John talked about butterfly valves in the car, and Van said he was going to put an apron on the snowplow. She thought they were nuts.

It's Sunday, and when I got up at 6:30, all I could see was swirling snow. The wind was howling and most of the windows were covered with snow. No Mass today for anyone who can't walk to church. Karen, Sally Brower and Rosie are out crawling through the drifts and having fun. Jinny shoveled the snow that Van couldn't reach with the plow. There was a four-foot drift by the South breezeway door and in front of the garage. Van has snow stuck in the horns on the plow so it's clear how high the snow was. A neighbor just called to say he thought he heard a fire siren, and I remembered that the "snow beast" sounds like a siren when Van really winds it up, so I told him I think that's what he heard.

Jinny invited the kids from her class to a skating party this afternoon 2 to 5. Nora and Jean Ann are going to supervise. They will have a fire on the ice and roast hot dogs and I'm making cocoa. Van plowed off the ice with the "Beast".

Van's plow, the "Beast"

Nora did have her senior dinner here Sunday and it was a success. Nine boys and 13 girls and Father Schrems also came. We had tomato juice, baked ham with pineapple rings, sweet potatoes, baked potatoes with butter and parsley, squash, whole green beans, pear and cheese salad, and apple pie and coffee. The ham weighed 12 ½ pounds. Nora did a great job of handling the group. We made graduate place-markers out of marshmallows and pipe cleaners. Except Van's, which was a fire chief with a can of beer, and Father Schrems with a purple and gold chasuble. We set the tables in our living room, using the Methodist church tables that are kept at the fire station. We almost had a problem when Dino came down to hunt them up because the Methodists suddenly decided to entertain some visiting ministers. Luckily, that dinner wasn't until Monday night and so we didn't have to dump the dishes and food. The group went off to a Rated A movie after dinner.

Nora's high school graduation picture

Karen and Rosie just wished on a week-old wish-bone. They both lost. Rosie had wished that all days would be school days, and Karen was glad she lost.

CHAPTER ELEVEN

LELAND VOLUNTEER FIRE DEPARTMENT
John K. Van Raalte

Leland Volunteer Fire Department 1950
Front: Rich Schlueter, Ben Hohnke, Harvey Schlueter, Herman Dunklow
Back: Chief Ernie Van Zee, John K. Van Raalte, Norman Price, Cliff Kilway, Donald Challender, Roy Buckler

Building the Department

When I was a young man in Holland, there was a fire at Macatawa Park, five miles from Holland on the Lake Michigan shore, and 24 cottages burned down. A couple of years later, there was a fire at Ottawa Beach, on the north side of the channel entrance to Black Lake (now Lake Macatawa), and a three-story wood hotel burned along with 12 cottages. One of the things I remember was going down to see the Ottawa Beach fire on my bike and seeing that the heat was so intense that four- and six-foot two-by-fours were floating up through the heat and coming down on the other side of the lake, so that they had to be extinguished where they dropped down. When I came up to Leland and realized that we had very little fire protection, I became interested in organizing an official fire department.

The same year that Luella and I were married, 1933, I got four people beside myself to come over to Greycote Cottage where we lived and we talked about doing something about fighting fires in Leland. At that time, Elmer Dalton had sold the village two 33-gallon sodi-acid fire extinguishers on wheels. There were 12 of us involved in getting a Fire Department started and our aim was to keep the membership small; only members that would actually do the job. No one got paid and so the fellows had to be really dedicated. At that point, all we had was 12 buckets and the two sodi-acid tanks. Originally we were just a bunch of fellows who had to learn what to do. I went downstate and over into Wisconsin, at my own expense, and talked with small fire departments about their problems and how they operated. At that point we just trained ourselves.

We found out the fire department at Paw Paw, Michigan, had an old Reo truck and they sold it to us cheap, for $150. If I remember right, it was a 1916 or 1918 model Reo, four cylinder engine. We took it to my garage and took the chemical tanks off. I built a 250-gallon water tank; then we bought a front-end mounted pump from Chicago, maybe a Darling pump. It was a combination low-pressure and high-pressure pump with a hose reel on it. We used that piece of equipment from 1933 until I came back from the Navy in 1946.

Ernie Van Zee with Reo Fire Truck

Then in 1946, we got an organization together, got donations, and bought a Reo chassis, new, on which we began to build a new fire truck. "We" was Harvey Schlueter, Roy Buckler, Herman Dunklow, Norman Price, Ernie Van Zee, myself and a few others. We worked three or four nights a week for two years, but not in the summer, from about 7 to 10 p.m. We built the entire truck. After the first winter's work, the Leland Township approved funds for fire protection. To begin with, this was completely voluntary; then the township built the fire station. It was used for the equipment and for meetings. Elder Blackledge designed the building. I told him to make it big enough so that the truck didn't just barely scrape inside. They built a meeting room behind, where the elections were held. That truck served us until the federal government released funds to small communities and donated fire equipment.

Then Leland got a big beautiful fire truck and we sold our truck to another village that needed it. The new truck was so heavy that you had to be really careful where you parked it and it was difficult to get to the water. We had to use portable pumps to get to the water.

Mrs. A. L. Bournique and John K. Van Raalte, Assistant Fire Chief christening new fire truck, July 1949

After the war the state sent a man, Wally Gannon, up here and to other small fire departments. He held meetings and trained small volunteer fire departments. Among the things he did was to set up practice fires. One fire we set up as part of the training was out at the north end of Lake Leelanau. We put down tar-paper and we took out five or ten barrels of old drain-oil from the garage and we poured kerosene on top of the drain oil and then we lit it. When it got to roaring and the black smoke and flames were up about 25 or 30 feet in the air, then our job was to see if we could put it out. Now that's an interesting experiment, because we put water on a pool of oil. What happens is that the water goes below, but the oil stays on top of the water and keeps on burning. So what you had to do was to cover the entire area as fast as you could to get the flame out. Invariably, there would be a little spot along the edge that would re-ignite. And then you'd start over. When you finally got it out, you'd be very, very happy. But you did learn how to put out an oil fire.

Then Gannon gave us training on indoor confined fires. The one important thing was, don't ventilate it. Don't get anybody with an ax to start chopping holes in the roof, because as long as the fire is confined, it will burn the oxygen up, and if you put in fog, it will go out. You'll have to stay there and watch it, because it will reignite. But the biggest mistake usually is to let it get ventilated. The only time I saw that done, as an absolute necessity, was when we had a fire just two blocks from where I lived. The house had been built and remodeled so there were at least three partial roofs beneath the existing roof; so the fire would get in under one roof, and there was no way to get at it except cutting a hole in the roof and getting the water down to it. Our son John was in charge of fighting that fire. They had used 18,000 gallons of water on the fire, but it was still burning in these false roofs. They were very fortunate that the wind was blowing away from any nearby houses.

Fire trucks in front of old Leland Fire Station

The fire alarm siren system in the early days consisted of three hard-wired alarm boxes, one at the Fire Station, one downtown, and one on the south end of town. They cycled differently, so anyone hearing it would go to that fire box and talk to the person who turned in the alarm. The system worked fairly well. For a number of years in the 1950s we used an alarm button that was installed right alongside of our bed at our house. A call would come in on the phone, I'd get dressed and Luella would blow the siren. Later, we got into radio equipment. To begin with, Dr. John Suelzer brought up the old equipment from Indianapolis to Leland. In the beginning, the sheriff wouldn't accept the calls, so we had to call Traverse City and their radio would alert us.

Some Fire Stories

One of the worst fires in early days was in East Leland. At that time migrant workers did all the cherry picking and they were housed in a big 3-door garage. They had a kerosene stove and the workers went out with one young girl left to mind a baby. We never knew what happened, but the building was totally aflame when we got there. The parents of the baby came up out of the orchard and I remember it took three men to stop the man and three more to stop the woman to keep them from going into this building. The building was totally aflame, the entire thing. The baby's body was finally found, and Mike Detzer, who wasn't even a fireman, went in and got the baby out. We got a blanket and we firemen wound up taking the body to the funeral home at Suttons Bay.

I especially remember another fire in a farmhouse building. It started in a basement where the owner had stacked the wood too close to the furnace. He called in the alarm and we got there. I went in the basement with a Scott Air Pack on; at first I couldn't see because it was all smoke. Finally I discovered the flame, but then I ran out of air. I knew it was a question of whether I would remain calm and cool and collected and get out of that building. So I got down on my hands and knees, because smoke tends to rise, and if you get down on your belly, you're apt to get fresh air. I started back for the door and I could hear the fellows talking back there, but I couldn't see and I wound up in what turned out to be a potato bin. I said to myself, "Now buddy, it remains to be seen if you're smart enough to get out of here. There is a way." I laid the nozzle down and I followed the hose back, hand over hand, on my knees back out the door. I got out the door with a choice comment about the bastard who put the Scott Air Pack back on the truck only partially full. Then I got another Pack and back in I went. The fire had started in the basement and I put that out. Lake Leelanau did a good job going upstairs, where the fire had gotten through a mopboard and set a couch on fire. They didn't destroy the whole upstairs with water; they actually threw the couch out and let it burn out in the front yard. But we made a new rule after that fire: anybody who put a Scott Air Pack back on the truck partially full was going to get skinned alive.

Then there was the one fire story that hit the national press. It happened because we had a hot water heater in a closet at the house and the ironing board was in that same closet. I came home for lunch one day and smelled some smoke. When I opened up the closet door, I found that the very top of the ironing board cloth was on fire. So I laid it down, grabbed my handkerchief and put the fire out, and said, "I'm in a hurry, I need to eat." We sat down at the table, and the next thing I knew, the smoke was coming out from under the table because my pants were on fire. So I got my pants off and into some water.

The event wasn't actually very exciting, but it happened that I was on jury duty that day and we had a long recess where we had to wait in a side room. To pass the time, I told the ironing-board story. Don Gordon, who was half-owner of the *Leelanau Enterprise* was there; the next thing I knew, the story was in the paper. Then UPI picked it up, and I started getting letters with copies of the story. Luella pasted the stories on a cardboard and framed it. People we knew all the way from San Francisco to Texas to Boston and Canada kept sending me copies. Each editor had the liberty to change the copy a bit. Most of the time, the story was told as a funny thing. But once in a while, the editor got sarcastic. So it turned out to be an interesting episode in the life of a small-town fire chief.

Firemen Cliff Kilway, John K. Van Raalte, Ernie Van Zee, Otto Hohnke & Roy Buckler posing in later years with retired 1918 truck

CHAPTER TWELVE

DEFENDING THE VAN'S GARAGE FLAGPOLE: 1962

John K. Van Raalte

When I bought the garage [112 S. Main St.] from the highway commission, it had a 35-foot steel flagpole in the grass triangle at the corner of Main and Cedar. We added the Mobil Oil sign. Then, in 1962 we were told that we had to move both as part of the highway beautification program because the highway department was taking all signs and poles off the right-of-way. That made me a little angry, but we poured a new foundation on our property and put the sign and flagpole back up. Then the highway folks sent a man who worked for the county road commission. He snuck around early in the morning before anybody was up and measured where the flagpole was on the property. After that, two big, fat-bellied men from the Cadillac office of the highway department came. They got out a cloth tape and measured from the centerline of the road to the flagpole and said that the flag would be three feet into the right-of-way when the wind blew from the west.

Now we were really mad. I said, "You know, you fellows don't bother me a particle. I spent three years of my life fighting for that flag, and it's on my property, and that's exactly where it is going to stay." I also told them, if they tried to take the flagpole down, I was the Fire Chief, and that I'd call a fire and have the entire fire department here and the *Leelanau Enterprise* would send down a photographer, and the *Traverse City Record Eagle* would send one too, and they'd be photographed with all the people present, making me take down the flag. They said, "Oh!" and that was the last I heard about not being able to fly the flag from the flagpole on my property!

Van's Garage Tow Truck circa 1955

CHAPTER THIRTEEN

WHY WE BECAME CATHOLIC

Luella M. Van Raalte - 1989

My father was brought up in the Swedish Lutheran faith in Sweden. My mother was brought up in the Methodist faith in Chicago. She and my father were married by a traveling minister. I do not know the minister's formal faith or name. My mother read her Bible daily and prayed to God for strength. I can still hear her quiet voice beseeching God to give her strength as life was hard in those days and also beseeching Him to watch over her husband and seven children.

From her example I learned early to pray. Since a Swedish Lutheran Minister only came around to the area maybe once a year, my Dad didn't go to church as he would not go to the German Lutheran Church. However the Swanson brothers who lived in the Good Harbor area finally persuaded my father to go to the Pilgrim Holiness Church which started having services in the Good Harbor area in the Kilway church (called that because Mose Kilway owned the property). My sister Minnie and I walked with our father three or more miles one-way in the summertime. In the wintertime it was not possible to walk because of the deep snow and my father felt that since the horses had worked hard all week they needed to rest on Sunday.

I didn't like the Pilgrim Holiness Revivals that were held in the summertime. The preachers urged everyone to come forward to the altar and kneel down and confess their sins because they might be killed on the way home and would go to hell. I was frightened, but much too shy to go forward and kneel and confess my sins with the other shouting and crying people, so I just quietly asked God to watch over me and He did. Fortunately my mother was a good example of Christianity even though she couldn't go to church. She taught us kindness, love of God and patience. She was a living example of all three virtues. Prayer and the Bible were her staff of life.

My sister Minnie, who was five years older than me, died of diphtheria the summer that she was fourteen years old. When fall arrived I had to walk alone through the woods and fields about two miles to go to school. As there were no neighbors to go with, my parents worried about me, especially in the wintertime. So I was sent to Leland to live with my sister Amelia and her husband, Henry Steffens. Since they were Lutheran I was plunged into Lutheranism, and went to the Lutheran Church and Sunday School. I wasn't sure that I liked it but it was better than the Pilgrim Holiness religion. Rev. Haesler had a daughter, Theodora, who was just about my age and lived just across the road and up the hill from my sister's home. We became great friends. Rev. Haesler would often take me home to the farm when he was on his way to the Good Harbor church and would pick me up on the way back or sometimes, if pre-planned, my father would take me back to Leland in a cutter which was enjoyable. Rev. Haesler often had to use a cutter also in the wintertime, but had a car to use when the roads were clear.

My sister Amelia rented rooms to make extra money. While I was there she rented a room to a girl from Gills Pier, Lucille Kolarik. Lucille had completed the 8th grade and had taken a course in Business and was working for the County Clerk, Ben Minsker, at the Courthouse in Leland. Lucille was a Catholic and she always went home on weekends.

One weekend she invited me to go home with her. It was such a happy, loving family; they welcomed me and made me feel right at home and they also made me feel that I was somebody important. They invited me to kneel down with them when the whole family said the rosary. On Sunday I went to Mass with them at St. Wenceslaus, Gills Pier. The Mass was in Latin and I was enthralled with the beauty of it although I didn't understand a word. It lit a spark in my heart that continued to burn through the years.

After that I was a frequent visitor in the Kolarik home and Lucille and I became very close friends. I continued to go to the Lutheran Church, took catechism lessons and prepared in due time for confirmation but my heart wasn't in it. I determined that some day I would be a Catholic (I didn't know how distant that day would be). On the day of confirmation when the class in unison pledged their faith in the Lutheran religion, I didn't say it because I didn't intend to remain a Lutheran.

When I was finishing the eighth grade I met Rita Hahnenberg at a get-together of all eighth graders in Leelanau County. We became very good friends. She invited me to her home and her family was another loving and happy Catholic family and they made me feel right at home. They were a musical family and I spent many happy hours with them. Sometimes I went to Mass at St. Mary's, Lake Leelanau. I especially liked midnight Mass at Christmas. The caroling and pageantry of the Mass were beautiful and enthralling. I felt close to God and felt a love that I had never felt before. However, although I felt drawn towards Catholicism, I lacked the courage to take the necessary steps to embrace the Catholic faith. I know that all of this time my good friends, the Kolariks and the Hahnenbergs, were praying for me but they knew that in God's own time it would happen. Never did any of them try to influence me, but their love for their faith showed clearly in their lives and was the biggest influence of all. My sister Amelia was very worried about my close association with Catholics and warned me not to get too involved. My parents didn't say anything, but I knew that they would be very upset if I became Catholic, so I continued going to the Lutheran Church, but also continued to be close friends with Lucille. I took part in the plays or played the piano for the plays that the Gills Pier Sodality put on, for which I was severely criticized by the Lutheran Minister. Lucille and I also went to dances at Gills Pier and had a great time.

Then in 1930 a handsome Dutchman appeared on the scene. He had been brought up in the Dutch Reformed Faith and was a regular attendant at church services when he lived in Holland. As a young boy he followed very strict rules on Sundays: no working, no movies, no fighting with his brother.

When Van came to Leland, he went to work for Carroll Stander at the garage on Main and Cedar that we later owned. One day I had to take my Dad's car down to the garage to get something done and I met the handsome Dutchman and thought he was very nice and that I would like to see him again. Well, I must have given him a good impression also as about a week later he called and invited me to go to a movie with him at Suttons Bay. I would like to have gone with him but I had a Walther League meeting that evening that I had to attend. I knew that he was lonesome and new in the area so I suggested that he take my niece, Helen, who was from Boyne City. Helen was about the same age as me. She was working at the Nicholas Hotel in Leland and we both were staying at my sister Amelia's home. So Van contacted her and she said OK. About a week later he called me again for a date and this time I could go so said yes. All the way to Suttons Bay he asked me questions about "Who lives in that house?" "Who owns that farm? I thought that he was terribly curious for a newcomer. When we finally reached Suttons Bay he turned to me and said, "Now I know that you are Luella! I thought that you and your niece Helen were playing tricks on me, but I knew that she, being from Boyne City, wouldn't know who lived in the various homes on this road." So right then I thought that he was a pretty smart guy and have never changed my mind. The confusion was caused by the fact that Helen and I resemble each other and, since my coat wasn't very nice, I had asked Helen if I could wear hers, and of course, she had worn it the week before. We have often chuckled about that since then.

Van and I were married in the Lutheran Parsonage by Rev. Schmidt. Van tried to go to the Lutheran Church but he didn't like it. The German Lutheran attitude irked him. He started an instruction class under Rev. Schmidt but didn't finish it because Rev. Schmidt was always talking about the evils of Catholicism. In fact he was a big help in eventually sending us to the Catholic Church because both Van and I knew that Catholics weren't as Rev. Schmidt pictured them. I continued to go to the Lutheran Church and John, Sara, Nora and Jinny were baptized in the Lutheran Church.

Then came the war. Although I had four children to take care of, without doing the bookkeeping for our business I had more time for myself and that meant more time to worry about Van. Suppose he was killed? What would happen to his soul since he spurned religion, that is, the Lutheran religion? Catholicism came back to haunt me, and I could almost feel my guardian angel tapping me on the shoulder and whispering "Why don't you do something about it?" but at that time I felt helpless.

After the war I'm sorry to say that once again Catholicism was pushed aside in the pressure of starting up the business again. My mother was ill and lived with us part of the time, so we drifted along as far as religion was concerned. A year later, Karen was born and I was presented with a problem. I believed firmly in baptism but I was no longer going to the Lutheran Church. So, when she was just a few months old and we were planning a trip to Holland, Michigan to see Van's mother, I baptized Karen myself! That allayed my worry about her soul should we be in an accident and killed.

Finally when Karen was a year or more old and my mother had died, Van and I took our courage in both hands and went to see Father Schrems at St. Mary's Lake Leelanau one evening. We were shaking in our boots but Father Schrems was so welcoming and so jolly that we felt right at home. After that we went once a week for instructions.

Bert & Lucille Kelsch and Luella & John K. Van Raalte

On April 16, 1949 we all were baptized conditionally into the Catholic Faith and Van, I, Johnny, Sara and Nora made our first communion the next day, Easter Sunday, not without incident however. The strain was too much for Nora so she felt faint and had to be taken out of church by Van. So after I returned from communion with Johnny and Sara, I went outside to stay with Nora while Van made his first communion and he had to march up at the tail end of the line. Father Schrems gave Nora communion after the Mass.

Our sponsors were Bert and Lucille (Kolarik) Kelsch and Fred and Agnes Hahnenberg. For many years after that we celebrated Easter and our conversion to Catholicism with Easter Sunday breakfast at the Kelsch's, with the table laden with food and everyone happy and laughing. Father Schrems usually was there also and Fred and Agnes Hahnenberg. It was a very joyful time.

In those days the Catholic Faith had many rules and regulations. Fasting from food and water from midnight to communion time; how virtuous one felt if one went to 10:00 A.M. Mass! Confessions frequently, once a week if possible. No meat on Friday, and strict fast and abstinence rules during Lent. Quite often a litany to the Sacred Heart, the Holy Spirit, the Blessed Virgin or the Saints was said after Mass and many times they were sung, which reminds me of a cute story. The response to one Latin Litany was "Libera nos a domini" and every time Sara's friend Susie heard it, she wondered why they would "leave her on a stormy day"! On First Fridays I used to get up at 5:00 A.M., kneel and say the Litany of the Sacred Heart in reparation for my sins and the sins of the world. I needed these rules and regulations and I felt that I was doing something concrete for my own salvation as well as others.

I was a true evangelist when we first became Catholic and wanted my Protestant relatives and friends to know about the joy I had found in Catholicism, and wanted them to experience it also. Needless to say, they were not at all enthusiastic and perhaps thought that I was a religious nut. I did have the delight of giving catechism lessons to two Leland girls, Barbara and Annette. This was done under Farther Voss' guidance. They reported to him periodically. He thought that with my Protestant background and the searching I had done I would be in a position to answer questions that they might feel free to ask me but not him. I also had the privilege of teaching religion classes at Gills Pier for several years; I felt that I was furthering God's love for mankind in my work. It gave me much joy to see my children receiving Holy Communion. My cup of happiness was full to over-flowing.

Van also was very active in the Church. He was a member of the Church Committee and he also was on the School Board. He was an usher for quite some time and always worked at the Annual Dinner as did I.

CHAPTER FOURTEEN

BOATS AND BOAT TRIPS

Luella M. Van Raalte

Going on a boat trip in September was the way Van could unwind after the busy summer season. He always had a love of boats, but money was very tight and we could not afford to buy one. In the early years, Van and John would borrow a fish tug and take a week-long trip on Lake Michigan. When John enlisted in the Navy, Van took the younger girls and me along on a fish tug vacation, but we were not enthusiastic about the fish smell and the huge brown spiders sharing our berth. In later years, Van borrowed boats from friends to take trips in a style that his wife and daughters would accept.

Trip to Wisconsin on the "Bonnie"

In September 1954 Van borrowed a very nice cabin cruiser, the "Bonnie", from his friend Pete Rennie in Traverse City. He wasn't sure about how much help I could be, so Van asked our friend, Gordon Dean, to come along to be First Mate for the trip. Jinny (11), Karen (7) and Rosie (3) went along on this trip. We went down the lakeshore to Ludington, across to Manitowoc, Wisconsin, up to Whitefish Bay and Washington Island and back across Lake Michigan to Leland.

The "Bonnie" with Luella, Jinny, Karen & Gordon Dean 1954

It was a great trip, all except for the last day, coming back to Leland when a thick fog closed in. Van knew that crossing the freighter shipping channel between the Manitou Islands and Leland could be dangerous in the fog. This was before radar and the only way that boats signaled each other was with foghorns. Soon we heard the deep blast of the foghorn from a freighter. Van cut the engine so that we could hear it better. We could hear the throb of the freighter's engine and knew it was nearby. Suddenly the freighter emerged from the fog bank right in front of us. It was so close that you could look up and see the men on the deck. We were all happy when we arrived safely back in Leland. I guess adventure is what I bargained for when I said, "I do" to this Dutchman!

The "Putt-Putt"

In 1959, our neighbors, the LaCameras, gave Van a 1906 boat that had been stored in their boathouse on the Leland River for 43 years. We called it the "Putt-Putt" from the sound the engine made. This is the story about that boat from the *Leelanau Enterprise*:

> "There are hundreds of boats on Lake Leelanau this summer, but probably the one which attracts the most attention is a 1906 inboard model owned by John K. Van Raalte of Leland. The boat was built that year by a Leland summer resident, Dr. I. N. Monfort, with the help of his son, Justin, now of Traverse City and Port Oneida, who was then in high school. She is made of cypress with white oak deck, is pointed at both ends and is held together with copper nails. Even after all these years, there isn't a sign of deterioration along her 18 foot, six inch length or four foot beam.
>
> Of even greater interest, especially for garageman Van Raalte, is her one cylinder, two cycle Kahlenberg engine, which operates on the first principle of gasoline engines. There are no spark plugs, no gears, no timing, no distributor, no camshaft. Ignition is accomplished by points which make and break in the combustion chamber.
>
> The boat and motor were stored at the Monfort family boathouse in Leland from 1916 until they were given earlier this summer to Van Raalte. The motor, in spite of its 43 year rest, started on the first turn and he has made no repairs or additions to either boat or motor."

Van, Jinny & Rosie in the "Putt-Putt"

Van enjoyed being out on the water and even took the Putt-Putt out on Lake Michigan, but eventually it was a little too slow and sedate for his style.

1960 – Ohio River Trip

Van was looking for another adventure so the 1960 family vacation trip with Jinny, Karen and Rosie was on a rented houseboat on the Ohio River. We picked up the boat in Kentucky, across the Ohio River from Cincinnati. It was a funny little flat-bottomed, snub-nosed boat with a 35hp outboard motor on the back. It was slow.

We motored along the edges of the Ohio River, watching the big barges go by. The first night we tied up at a private dock with a bar. The noise from the bar kept us awake for hours and Van wasn't sure it was such a safe place to be. After that we found places at night where we could nose the boat into the shore. We would tie the bow to a tree on shore and then use the anchor at the stern to pull the boat a little offshore so that someone couldn't climb onboard while we were sleeping.

Houseboat rented for Ohio River Trip

Just past Warsaw, Kentucky, we had to go though our first lock, the Markland Locks and Dam. We approached and gave the signal for entry, a long horn blast followed by a short one. Then we waited for the lockmaster to signal us to go through. He let us in with a Coast Guard ship that had been working on buoys. We tied up to the floating mooring posts and "locked though" successfully. We were very proud of ourselves.

When we got to Madison, Indiana, we decided it was time to turn around and head back. We didn't anticipate how much slower our boat would be going upstream against the current. The only way to make it back in time was to put in longer days. We got up at the crack of dawn, but there was a river mist in the mornings before the sun was warm enough to burn it off. Jinny got the job of sitting at the front of the boat and being the lookout for floating logs in the river. We made it back in time and we thoroughly enjoyed our river adventure.

Learning to Sail

A big expense in boating was gasoline, so Van decided to give sailing a try. He found a sailboat that had been sitting unused and bought it for a very reasonable price. Our friend, Bill Steel, wrote this recollection:

> *"Van has had another love besides Luella – boats; boats with special features. They had to be ancient, inexpensive, and they had to require mammoth amounts of work. My association with this aspect of Van's life came about because sailing was new to him and I'd been doing it most of my Leland life. So he came to me for advice (a real switch, since it was usually I going to him for mechanical expertise!), both on outfitting the C-Scow he had acquired and some of the basics of sailing.*
>
> *Sitting in the river, that boat soaked up only enough water to seal the bottom cracks. So whenever the boat heeled, water gushed in the side cracks. Not being keen on suicide, I sailed in this boat only once. We could always tell if the wind was over 20mph, for Van and John would be whizzing madly across Lake Leelanau in that jib-rigged C-Scow – the only one so equipped in the world! We'd watch them with awe at their fantastic speed and reckless sailing, and with fear that they would sink or tip over, but they always made it back."*

Van, Nora & John D. sailing on Lake Leelanau

Purchase of the Seabee and First Trip - 1971

While he continued to borrow boats for yearly trips, Van had his eye on a 1938 Richardson cabin cruiser owned by Mr. Kuhn, a summer resorter who hadn't used it for several years. They finally struck a deal for $1,400, which was a price that we could handle and so a dream of his was realized. Van worked early and late to get the boat ready for a short trip and we christened it the "Seabee." The Seabee was 26' long, had a small kitchen and dining area and a couple of beds. This boat had led a sheltered life so far, docked in a boathouse on the Leland River and taken for sedate cruises on Lake Leelanau. The old gal had no idea what exciting adventures were ahead of her.

The "short" trip that Van wanted to take in September would be the boat's first trip out on Lake Michigan. Since I always enjoyed our boat trips, Van did not have too much trouble persuading me to go along, but as a clincher he said, "Since I'm not too familiar with the boat, we'll hug the shore line and go only to Charlevoix." I listened, knowing full well that his adventurous spirit would never be satisfied with that. It wasn't. We got to Charlevoix in four hours. At Charlevoix, Van said, "It's so nice, and you have never seen the Les Cheneaux Islands, how about taking a quick run up there?" I didn't object.

It was a six-hour run up to the dock at Hessel on the south shore of the Upper Peninsula. I went up to buy a few groceries. When I got back to the boat, I put my groceries and handbag in but the rope tying the boat to the dock had a little too much slack in it. As I went to step in, the boat drifted away from the dock, and into the water I went. I came up sputtering and grabbed a post on the dock and yelled. From somewhere a man came running and helped pull me out. When Van got back he saw all the dripping clothes on the back deck and he said "What the hell are you washing clothes for NOW?" After he got over the first shock of my explanation, we had a good laugh.

On our return trip, Van followed along the shoreline of the UP into Naubinway Marina before heading south to Beaver Island. All was fine for a while, but then the wind picked up, and what a beating we took. The waves were monstrous. My stomach was tied in knots. I never prayed so hard! Van is a very skilled Captain; he would cut the engine and we would slide over the big waves, then rev it up until another one came. Sometimes the water just deluged the windshield and it was impossible for the wiper to keep up and we would hit a wave hard. Wham! It shook the whole boat and I was scared that the bottom would break apart. I prayed that the engine wouldn't quit because we would never have been able to keep the boat out of the trough and we would have capsized. The anchor, which was up on the front deck, came loose and nearly came through the windshield. I had to take the wheel and steer over the waves while Van got the anchor in. After five hours of this we finally came to Beaver Island. Never did good old terra firma look so good.

The next day, the wind and waves subsided, and we took off for Charlevoix; the waves this time really were moderate and our trip home to Leland was uneventful.

Trip down the Mississippi on the Good Ship "Seabee" – 1972

Since we had enjoyed the Ohio River trip, Van started planning a trip on the Mississippi River. Ernie Van Zee made canvas enclosures for the back deck and the Seabee looked quite elegant and was much more functional. Van scraped, sanded, rebuilt and painted the boat and went over the engine piece by piece. All was a work of love. We cast off on Saturday, September 9, 1972.

Van on the Seabee in the Leland Harbor

We headed down the Michigan shoreline to Chicago. Our grandson JP joined us for the Leland to Holland leg of the trip with overnight stops at Manistee and Pentwater. Other than five foot waves, an engine miss that needed attention, and some thick fog, it was a good trip. Well, except for the first night when I almost set the boat on fire. There are five steps for lighting the alcohol stove, but I bypassed one of them. As a consequence flames leapt two feet high! Fortunately Van was around to put out the fire. Needless to say, I was shaken so we started over with Van lighting the stove, which he has done ever since. Later in Chicago we saw a boat burned down to the water line from an alcohol stove fire. We were fortunate and duly impressed with the importance of correct operation and caution.

When we got to Holland we were able to dock on Lake Macatawa very near where Van's sister, Dora lives. JP's family picked him up. I think he would have liked to continue on with us, but he had to get back to school.

Leaving Holland in the morning, we had an 8-foot following sea. Van threw out a sea anchor (a bucket on a rope) to keep the boat from broaching. We put in at South Haven for a break. Being chicken-hearted I was all for staying there the night, but Van decided that we should push on. I had complete confidence in his ability but also had knots in my stomach. We made it to St. Joseph harbor for the night. Being on the boat is sometimes like camping. It rained hard that night and in the early morning Van woke up with the bottom part of his bed soaking. He wrapped his feet in dry towels and went back to bed.

Our friend Remi Gits had a berth for us at Jackson Park Harbor, Chicago. Instead of a dock, this harbor had buoys tie-ups. Remi was there to meet us, and we came ashore in a dinghy and had dinner at a nearby restaurant on Lake Shore Drive. The next day, Remi, two of his children and a friend of his joined us for the trip down the Chicago Ship Canal. It was very interesting to see the heart of Chicago from a boat.

It took nearly five hours on the Chicago Ship Canal to get to Willow Springs where Remi lives. After dinner at his home, when we returned to the Seabee, Van decided that he didn't like the mooring. We were tied to a rock wall in the canal and he thought that if two barges met there our boat might not fare too well. So we continued on downstream and tied up to a barge already moored in a docking area. I worried all night that another barge might come in. Every time a barge went by on the canal I jumped up to find out if they were turning in. I didn't have a restful night. Also the barge we were tied to was filled with partially rotted corn, which emitted quite an odor.

The Chicago Ship Canal joined the Des Plaines River at Joliet, Illinois. On our way there, we had to go through our first lock of the trip and we came across a barge that had come loose from its mooring and nearly blocked the river. In early afternoon we had to wait an hour or so because there was a speed boat race up ahead. Then there was another lock. We waited some more. Finally seven or eight small boats all were able to enter the lock with a towboat, a tight squeeze but we all got through. We anchored overnight in the Mazon River. WOW! The mosquitoes! We went through three locks that day and spent three hours waiting so didn't make very good mileage.

Monday, Sept. 18: Thinking about Nora on her birthday today. We are on the Illinois River now. We stopped at Marseilles, Illinois, and the small grocery store there reminded me of the Leland Merc. We docked at Chillicothe, Illinois, for the night. No services except gas. A man and a boy were fishing and had several catfish, which they gave to us and Van cleaned.

We made our way down the Illinois River and through Lake Peoria through periods of heavy fog, then wind and rain. After an overnight at Havana, the next day was so hot (96 degrees) that we had to anchor and take a siesta at Wilson Island. Arrived at Kampsville but found no adequate docking facilities. A lady said that we could dock at a private dock, but the dock looked as if we would pull it right out into the channel if a wind came up. A ferry runs from one shore to the other here and Van decided to dock south of the ferry ramp by throwing out two anchors. We were wakened at 4 a.m. by a storm. In the morning we found that the wind had pushed us ashore. Van studied the situation and by maneuvering the two anchors and walking in mud up to his knees he managed to get us free. As he was pulling up the rear anchor, he suddenly had only rope. The anchor had chafed through the rope and it was in the mud in the Illinois River. He moved the boat to the private dock and went to get a small boat to do some fishing for the anchor, but no luck.

We reached a major milestone today, the confluence of the Illinois and Mississippi Rivers. The current was strong and the wind was blowing, but we docked successfully at a Marina just north of Veteran's Bridge, St. Louis. The dockage fee was steep ($5.20), we didn't have electricity and the toilet was quite a ways away. After we docked a man in a canoe swung in behind us and tied up. We had passed him previously in the "Chain of Rocks Canal." He is from Winona, Minnesota, and is paddling down the Mississippi River to New Orleans. We thought we wouldn't sleep that night because there were barges on the river side and a railroad train on the bank side, a highway bridge ahead and helicopters landing on the marina roof, but we were tired and it didn't bother us at all.

On Friday we got to Bussen Trautman's quarry 13 miles south of St. Louis, where Bill Ebenreck [Sara's father-in-law] had reserved a spot for us. We went under the St. Louis Arch. At the quarry, the owner "Turk" showed Van where to moor the boat and then gave us his car to use. We had a lot of errands to run so this was very helpful. We ate our meals with Bill, Mary, Paul and Judy Ebenreck and spent both Friday and Saturday nights there.

Monday, Sept. 25: It was raining and foggy but we left as we would have been in the way had we stayed longer. We strained our eyes to see buoys and day markers. After five hours we tied up to a dock at Chester, Illinois. There are no marinas between St. Louis and Cape Girardeau, so one has to just keep on going or tie up at a small dock. Just as we turned in our wiper blade broke off. Van went uptown in Chester to buy a replacement. We were tied tight to the dock but the dock didn't look very secure and I was afraid that the weight of our boat would pull it loose and that boat and dock and me would go swirling down the river. So I stood ready with an anchor just in case until Van returned. It rained so hard that afternoon and the visibility was so poor that we got permission to tie up to a towboat. This is the kind of weather that makes one say, "Why in the hell didn't I stay home"!

The next day finally was a clear day and we had an easy trip down to Cape Girardeau, Missouri, arriving mid-morning. The marina there was a long floating dock with gas, water and electricity. There is a twenty-foot cement wall on the east side of the city to protect it during flood stages of the Mississippi River. A long walk leads from the dock to the wall and then metal steps lead to the top where there is a small platform. We called Mrs. Findley, grandmother of our son-in-law John Logan, Jinny's husband. Mrs. Findley came down and took us to her home. It is a stately brick house with stained glass windows. Mrs. Findley said that there were seven fireplaces in it when they bought it, now there are only four. In the living room is a nearly life sized portrait of Mrs. Findley over the fireplace. After lunch, she had made an appointment for a Cape Girardeau Bulletin reporter to interview us on our trip and take pictures. Then she took us on a tour of the city. We drove past the College where Mrs. Findley taught biology and chemistry. We drove past St. Vincent's Cathedral. This was one of the first Catholic Parishes established west of the Mississippi. We stayed at Cape Girardeau overnight.

We had 52 miles to the confluence of the Mississippi and the Ohio rivers. On one horseshoe turn we met a barge and towboat with a load seven barges long, five wide, and with two towboats; the biggest one we have ever seen. We left the Mississippi River and turned up the Ohio River at noon. The waters of the Ohio are green, quite a change from the muddy brown Mississippi. The Mississippi is full of eddying currents but the Ohio River was quiet. The sun came out and we had an enjoyable trip. We hoped to reach Paducah, Kentucky, so that we could get charts, but ended up tying up to a barge. Every night I appreciate the Lake Michigan marinas. Have only found two marinas since Lake Michigan and one only had gas, water and electricity. No toilets or showers. Our tempers were a bit short tonight and Van hit the sack right after eating dinner, which I had to prepare, and also had to do the dishes. It was too long a day for a work day and much too long for a vacation day.

The next day was sunny but chilly. The ceiling of the boat dripped from moisture condensation. We headed upstream against the current. We had to take a detour up the Tennessee River to get gas and supplies. In the afternoon, the engine developed a miss. We stopped and Van replaced the coil. While we were anchored a thunderstorm hit and it just poured. When we reached the Golconda lock there were two barges ahead of us so we decided to stop for the day. We pulled up into a little stream with a sandy bottom and shore. We waded ashore, walked on the sand and I picked up some pretty stones. It was a lovely, quiet and peaceful spot. We slept well. All we heard was the gentle lapping of the waves and the shush, shush of the bow as it nudged the sandy shore.

Getting through locks is a challenge! At Golconda, one barge was in the lock, one was waiting to go upstream, one was tied up by the mooring blocks waiting and two were waiting to come downstream. We circled and signaled hoping that the lockmaster would let us in with one of the barges, but no luck. Finally Van got the boat close to a ladder on the lock approach wall. He climbed up and went to the lock master to find out when we could expect to go through. He said in about an hour but it was noon before we got the signal to proceed. It took only about ten minutes to lock through and we were on our way.

The following day, there were more locks to navigate. At lock #49 barges were lined up and we stopped to talk with a towboat crew. They had been waiting since 4 a.m.! They invited us aboard to have coffee. We ended up waiting three hours to lock through. There was a lot of current and strong winds so Van did some tall maneuvering to keep us in the right position. I don't want to ever see a lock again, but there are five more between here and Madison. Tonight we are docked at someone's floating houseboat. No one is here so we are hoping it is ok. There are no public docks at Uniontown, just a ferry ramp.

Sunday, Oct. 1: No rain but the temperature was only 40 degrees. The alcohol stove warmed up the cabin nicely. We stopped and went to Mass at Mt. Vernon, Indiana. Arrived at Lock # 48 in mid-afternoon and we were able to go right through. At 4 p.m. we saw a big marina; thought it was a mirage! It is the Plaza Yacht Club Marina. It has gas, electricity and water, showers, and a store so we docked for the night. The owner let us use his car to drive into Evansville, Indiana, about 5 miles, to get supplies.

On Monday the river was as calm as a mirror. The sun cast a rosy haze on everything. A jet trail was golden instead of white. The day that started out at 52 degrees ended up at 80 degrees. Got through two more locks without trouble and traveled 62 miles. At 5pm we found a little creek and docked there for the night. Van had a nightmare. He dreamed that there was a flood and our boat pulled loose from its mooring and was pushed downstream banging against rocks until there was very little left of it. I was in the water but I had a life jacket on so was okay. He was glad to wake up. The dream was so real that he had to get up and check whether the boat was still securely moored.

At Cannelton, Indiana, five barges were waiting at the lock. We circled where the lockmaster could see us, while keeping out of the way of the barges. Those captains were impatient at being held up so long. I began to worry that Van's nightmare was a premonition of what might happen to our boat among all these barges. After two hours Van decided that I should try to get ashore and find out what the scoop was from the lockmaster since he had ignored all of our requests for entry, but I chickened out. I would have had to use our boarding ladder and the water was deep right up to the edge and then there was a steep stony slope to climb. It looked too hazardous to me. I told Van that I was a 63-year-old woman, not a fifteen-year-old kid. So we waited and circled and circled and waited. All of the traffic was going downstream and we didn't understand why he couldn't lock us through when he had to raise the water to get another barge. We not only watched the light but also watched the men because at some locks they would wave us in without changing the light to green. After waiting a total of 5 hours we got through. We traveled ten more miles and then pulled into Clover Creek at Cloverport, Kentucky for the night.

Going upstream, we chugged along at 7 miles per hour. This stretch of the Ohio River meanders north, east, north, west, east and south. It took us 9 hours to get from Cloverport to Brandenburg which would take 1 hour by car. Since we had run 16 miles yesterday, idled 5 hours at the lock, and traveled 65 miles today we were concerned that we would run out of gas before we reached Brandenburg, but we made it. We found a floating raft with gas tanks, but the raft was broken and half under water and the tanks were leaning at a precarious angle. There was no visible walk from the shore and our hearts sank. Then a man drove up in a pick-up. We called to him and asked if we could get gas and he said "Sure!" He pulled himself up to the raft in a small boat and pumped 44 gallons for us. We anchored by a new launching ramp.

Thursday, Oct. 5: Van started up the engine, pulled in the anchor, and put the boat in reverse but the boat didn't budge. He put on full power and nothing happened. I sat at the controls while Van got out and pushed, first just his own weight and then with a 2x4 for leverage. We didn't budge. The problem was that the river went down six inches overnight and we didn't have that much depth to spare. Van walked uptown to a garage. The man said, "There is no way to get you out, I only have 25 foot of cable." So Van explained how he could do it by using a snatch block and said he would buy 200 foot of special cable, which he did at a cost of $25.00. The man got his wrecker in place and his snatch block ready while Van did the legwork. At first it looked like it wasn't going to budge, but in a few minutes it came loose. We paid the garage man $30.00. It was an expensive morning.

The afternoon was sunny and warm. The river winds through high walls of rock on both the Indiana and Kentucky sides. We could see cattle grazing on the top of hills. We anchored west of the Alpine locks near the outskirts of Louisville. Van woke up at 4 a.m. to see a barge nosed into a bank to the right of us. They will nose into the bank while waiting to lock through. This was a little close for comfort. It was very foggy, but we moved out anyway as soon as it was light and cautiously started up the river. Between the fog and more waiting at the lock we only made 10 miles the whole day. We docked at a marina at Jeffersonville, Indiana across the river from Louisville.

Saturday, Oct. 7: We talked it over and decided that it was time to end this boat trip adventure. We arranged for docking and for a car ride home. A while later our son-in-law, John Logan, went with Van and they towed the Seabee back to Leland. This trip was an adventure of a lifetime!

July 1978 North Channel Boat Trip in the Seabee
John K. Van Raalte

I wanted to take a summer boat trip up to Canada. My brother Al said he would go, daughter Karen said she would go for the first leg, and grandson JP planned to join us later. We had a perfect day with calm winds going up to Beaver Island and we anchored out in the harbor south of the ferry channel. That evening a sailboat pulled into the harbor, heading back from the Chicago to Mackinac race. From the sounds of their laughter, they were having quite a good time. We watched them motor south in the harbor while taking the sails down and we knew what was about to happen but couldn't do anything about it. Their keel hit the bottom as soon as they went past the dredged ferry channel. There was a lot of colorful language that drifted across the water when they went aground.

The next day the barometer dropped and the wind picked up. The weather report was for increasing wind so we decided to stay put. At one point, we ventured out far enough to check the sea, but it was too rough to take off.

Overnight fog rolled in, but the barometer started coming up which meant improving weather. After lunch we left the harbor but the engine started missing badly. While I worked on the engine, more fog rolled in. At that point, Karen decided that she would abandon ship and take the ferry to the mainland. I think she figured that I was going to go out in the fog (which, of course, I was) and she didn't want to do it. I think she would have enjoyed the trip after the fog lifted, going north to Sault Ste. Marie.

The weather report kept calling the fog "patches," but it was sure a big fog-patch. It was so thick that we were within 50 feet of the Gray's Reef light before we saw it. By using the depth sounder and reading the charts, I could determine what part of the reef we were on. Finally we saw the shore and we headed north following the contour of the land. We came under the Mackinac Bridge at 9:00 p.m. I was blowing the fog signal as we crept further looking for the marina. Some young people called out, "Just a little further." We sailed on in but the slips were full so the harbormaster instructed us to just anchor offshore within the harbor. We poured a drink, got something to eat, and went for a walk. What a day!

The Les Cheneaux Islands blend into each other, so you are almost to the entrance of a harbor before you can pick it out. We made stops at Hessel, Cedarville, DeTour Village and arrived at Sault St. Marie where we met Luella and JP. We went up to the locks and watched freighters go through, something Luella hadn't seen before. JP joined the crew and Luella drove back to Leland.

We headed east and then south along Sugar Island, through Lake George. We tried some fishing but got nothing. We saw some splashing in the reeds, so JP and Al took the dinghy and rowed over. They found some enormous carp. JP tried to get one, not successfully, but they had a lot of fun trying. The bulk of the lake is 4 to 7 feet deep, with a 10 mile long dredged channel about 25 feet wide down the middle. It is evident from all the markings and the dredging that this channel is used by something other than passenger craft, but we didn't see anything else. There are hundreds of islands that make it an interesting navigational challenge. About a mile after leaving Lake George, we came to the intersection of the up bound channel going to the Sault and the St. Joseph channel, which is the waterway between the Canadian mainland and St. Joseph Island. The St. Joseph channel is both an interesting and a difficult navigation feat because it twists between rocks and other features. There was a fixed bridge across from St. Joseph to the mainland with a vertical clearance of 8 feet on the south and 12 feet on the north. I finally made the decision to try it. Otherwise we'd have to backtrack. I didn't want to risk heading south in the up bound freighter channel and it was going to be difficult to get across to the down bound channel. The St. Joseph channel was narrow and twisting, with enormous boulders to navigate around, but the bridge turned out to be high enough to not be a clearance problem. Shortly after passing the bridge, we came to an island called Campement d'Ours Island. We ran around behind it and found a beautiful cove, got an anchorage and went back to some fishing. JP had a pike follow his line in, but he didn't get it.

Leland postcard showing the Seabee second from the right

We were running in the North Channel along the Canadian shoreline. We went by an abandoned town called Bruce Mines and into Thessalon. There was a sawmill on the bay and the watchman there was glad to show us around. They specialized in birch plywood. The core of the trunk, not good for plywood, was taken to another mill and made into chips sold for paper. The town of Thessalon appeared to be dying. The streets were littered with trash and a bunch of young punks hung out there. It was a lonesome, weird spot. The sawmills had pulled out and the only industry left was this one plywood place. In that part of Canada, industry is either related to lumber or mining.

The next day we went on down to Blind River, where I'd been once with Nick Lederle. The inner harbor was tricky, with some pilings about two feet under the surface of the water - and only by sheer luck did we miss them. JP and Al went uptown to buy supplies and I worked on charting the next phase of the trip. I decided to head for a spot on Aird Island called Little Detroit. With JP on board, it was a cinch because I could do navigation, and JP and Al could switch off at the wheel. That evening we actually caught enough small fish for a meal. We had the dingy and rode around into some little coves in the harbor. The shoreline is all rock. We saw several beavers hauling tree-limbs over to their lodge.

From Little Detroit we headed to the Little Current. JP and Al walked to town to stock up. We kept needing supplies because we didn't have room to store much and the icebox wouldn't hold much. We had to buy ice for it every chance we got. Block ice was easy to get because so many sailboats also need it. We got a bottle of liquor, but when Al was down below, he knocked it into the sink. It smashed and went down the drain into the lake. So I suggested they get their fish poles out since the fish might be drunken enough that we could catch a couple. They had gotten a pie, but it was a frozen blueberry pie and we had no way to bake it on an open burner. I tried it in a cast-iron frying pan. So we ended up eating the blueberries, after scraping off the crust.

On Wednesday the 26th we dropped anchor at Little Beaver Harbor and caught more fish here than anyplace on the trip. We got perch, rock bass, sunfish and two bullheads. The barometer was dropping, so we stayed in that little bay which was excellent protection from wind from any direction. Five boats were fishing, all on the same spot. Thunderstorms did eventually roll in.

The next day we went by Centre Island, Badgeley Island, and George Island and then to Kilarney. The scenery is high and rocky and beautiful. Kilarney was a destination for yachts and has high-class marinas and hotels and other facilities. There were a number of restored old boats there. Then we headed to Heywood Island and began the trip back home.

CHAPTER FIFTEEN

MARYLAND LOGGING ADVENTURE: 1979
John K. Van Raalte

Preparing to go Logging

After I retired, I starting making the trip to the Manitou Islands with Pete Jurica on his logging barge and I learned a lot about logging techniques. For several years I had wanted to make a trip to Prince Frederick, Maryland, to cut firewood for our daughter Sara and her husband, Clyde Ebenreck. They have a lot of land with a lot of trees, but there were many angles to consider about how to get there with the equipment I'd need to get the logging done. Their property slopes off beyond the house and yard into a deep ravine. I was going to need a piece of heavy equipment to do that work.

I started with an old Ford 4-wheel drive pickup. The body was rusted out. I riveted sheets of galvanized metal into the big holes and filled small holes with putty. I mounted an old camper top on the back of the truck. It took me a week to get a 6' top to fit onto the 8' truck box. I spent one whole day sanding and cleaning the truck and masking everything that wouldn't be painted. John did the painting and it came out looking beautiful. I added a new trailer hitch for the camper trailer that John was loaning us. Had to buy an electric winch, and then had to remove the snowplow mount on the front bumper and replace it with a bumper that would hold the winch. Finally I added another battery to run the winch.

For logging tools I borrowed a cant hook from Pete Jurica, got 400 feet of spooled steel cable, a piece of chain, a snatch block, cable-clamps, 3 chain saws, a grinder for sharpening the saw, a six-pack of outboard oil to mix with gasoline, a container for gasoline, containers for oil, couple pairs of gloves, my working clothes, my hard hat, a portable radio, and a set of ear protectors to deaden the sound of the chainsaws. Finally, I was equipped and ready to go! Luella is the navigator, so she got the maps and all the travel supplies ready.

Happenings on the Highway

We started out in early October. The pickup pulled nicely, but steered terribly. It should have had power steering to handle the radial tires, but it didn't. On the second day we pulled into a travel plaza to gas up and eat lunch. When I went back to start the truck, it was no go. The batteries were dead. Travel plaza attendants have only a vague idea that an auto has wheels so were no help. Finally someone gave us a jump-start. At the next exit we found a service station and a test showed that the alternator wasn't working. With our headlights on, and running our defroster and wipers because it was raining, the load made the batteries go dead. It would cost $65 for a new alternator but a new battery only cost $45, so the attendant charged the new battery up partially, and after an hour we took off again. Then we got into the section of the Pennsylvania turnpike where they're doing a lot of repair work, so the signs said "turn on the lights" and there went the battery lower. In a tunnel, you have to turn on the lights also, so I was using a lot of lights in daylight, but we obeyed the law. When we stopped for the night, I went to a service station and recharged the batteries again. That got us the rest of the way. John shipped an alternator and an ammeter to me. Until it arrived, each night I would put my batteries on Clyde's 6-amp charger. Then when I was working up close to the house, I'd have the battery charging all the time that I was using it.

Logging a Winter's Wood

As I'd remembered, all the land is downhill from the house, no matter which direction you go. There was a persimmon tree by the garage, so I put the snatch block there and hooked the cable on. Then the weight of the pickup going down hill with the cable was sufficient to pull the logs up at the other end of the cable. This saved the electric winch and brought the logs up quickly. If a log weighed 2,000 pounds and the pickup weighed 6,000, you have a 3 to 1 advantage. The laws of gravity help out.

I'd usually wait until about 10 a.m. before starting work because there was heavy dew and the grass would be slippery so I couldn't drive the truck downhill. I discovered that the under soil, which is a combination of clay and crushed rock, is very, very slippery if you're trying to get back uphill. It reminded me of trying to go into the forest at Nora's; you also don't do that if it's raining.

Van with chainsaw at Sara's

One tree I dropped was growing next to a ravine a couple hundred feet deep. I tied the tree to a stump and the rope held, so it didn't go down into the ravine. I dragged some treetops up to the house and our grandson Jered (6) had a good time fooling around on the tree limbs. One oak that I cut was leaning about 30-degrees from vertical. It split on me about 15 feet up with an awful roar. Luella was down there as safetyman for me, so she got a picture as I was cutting it. It was a dangerous operation and I got nervous, but we got the tree down.

Sara and Clyde had a little cat that had wandered into the place just a couple days before we got there which we named Frisky. I tried very hard to get them to give me the cat because I got very attached to it. He was all white with patches on his knees, and was the friendliest thing you've ever seen with the loudest purr for a little kitten. You could hear it about ten feet away. Luella got the chore of housebreaking the cat, because it decided to do its duty on the davenport, which no one seemed to approve of. She finally got it litter-box trained.

Luella stacking wood at the Ebenrecks in Maryland

There was a table and bench out back of the house that was a nice place to sit. While we were out there, even in October, one day it was 94-degrees and another it was 84. It would be cold in the morning and then warm up. It didn't really rain. That was marvelous because rain would have been a disaster for the logging operation. Clyde and I worked together chain sawing and splitting the wood. Luella did a lot of wood piling. We got a lot of trees cut down, sawed into pieces, split and stacked. Not bad for a 70 year old couple!

CHAPTER SIXTEEN

TRIP TO PORTLAND AND SAN FRANCISCO: 1980
Luella M. Van Raalte

In April 1980, Van's sister Dora Schurman and I took a trip to Oregon and California. I drove the Rambler to Rockford, Michigan. Jinny and John gave me a tour of their new house on Big Brower Lake and I had a great visit with my grandchildren, Marie and Jason. Their home is beautiful. The next morning Dora and I met at the Grand Rapids airport and were off to Portland.

Nora met us at the airport. She zipped through the Portland traffic like a pro and headed to the Malloy ranch in North Plains. The next day, we went to Forest Grove and visited with Van's uncle Dewey Keeler and his wife. They are part of the Keeler relatives that Van visited on his trip to Oregon in 1926 and Dora had never met them. In the afternoon Nora gave us a grand tour of Portland. That night Nora and I sat up and talked until 1:30 a.m. Oregon time.

That week we took Hwy 30 to the coast and were able to see Mt. St. Helens. It had become active that month, producing steam and other volcanic activity. The black ash coating the side of the mountain was visible to the naked eye. We drove along the

Columbia River to Astoria, then walked down to the ocean and watched the waves rolling in and looked for sand dollars. People were digging for clams while we were there. We drove back on Hwy. 26 through the Tillamook Burn. Another day, Nora took us and her mother-in-law, Blanche Malloy, on a trip to Multnomah Falls and beyond that to the Bonneville Dam on the Columbia River. She took the old scenic route, the same one that Van used in 1926 on his trip to Oregon.

On Sunday we flew to San Francisco, the fabulous city I'd always read about and one which I had dreamed of seeing some day. Karen's third floor walk-up apartment was at 351 Cornwall St. and was large and comfortable. We had dinner at a nearby Vietnamese restaurant, the Golden Turtle.

Over the next week, Karen showed us San Francisco and the neighboring areas. In Muir Woods some trees are 250 feet in height and 17 feet in diameter. Karen drove on Hwy 1. It is mountainous and has curves and switchbacks that reminded me of Mexico. We saw laurel and eucalyptus trees and they smelled so good. We stopped at Stinson Beach and walked on the shore a bit but it was very windy and chilly. We rode the cable car on California Street.

While walking around the path at the Coit Tower we saw a young Chinese man doing Tai Chi, a rhythmic slow motion exercise. We shopped at the Embarcadero Center and at Fisherman's Wharf. We saw the view from the 27th floor of the Transamerica Building. We went to Chinatown, walked on Lombard Street, stopped at Russian Hill, did the Alcatraz tour and drove through Golden Gate Park. The flowers there were beautiful; big, pink rhododendrons and many beds of pansies of all colors. We went to the Museum of Science and to the Japanese Gardens. We saw the Presidio Military Complex that covers a large beautiful area and the Palace of Fine Arts that was built for the early 1900's World's Fair. It withstood the big earthquake and is a beautiful edifice. Fort Point, under the Golden Gate Bridge, was built in 1853 and also survived the 1906 earthquake.

On Saturday, we had almond paste "wonder" rolls from a nearby Chinese bakery, then drove north to Sonoma Valley for some winery tours. Afterwards we stopped in Santa Rosa to see Barbara (Gibson) & Elliot Norwood. Barbara is my godchild and although she has been back to Leland several times since her marriage I had never met her husband, Elliot, so this was a happy occasion. On our trip back to the city we saw the famous fog rolling in under the Golden Gate Bridge.

The next day it was time to leave, and so we left this beautiful and exciting city. Both Dora and I felt enriched by having seen it and sampled some of its excitement. We were grateful to both Karen and Nora for having given of their time and of themselves to make our trip so enjoyable.

CHAPTER SEVENTEEN

MOUNT ST. HELEN'S ERUPTION

John K. Van Raalte

View of the Malloy ranch

Just like in previous trips to Oregon and our trip to Maryland, my plan for our 1980 visit to the Malloy ranch in Oregon was to cut firewood. We actually got more wood cut in the first week than I ever did before. We were cutting just east of the house, so we had only about a thousand feet to haul it up to the woodpile, which is easy. Our work was progressing very rapidly until Mt. St. Helen erupted and the whole area got a quarter-inch of ash.

On Sunday the wind dropped and rain had settled the ash, so we went back to logging. For the last three years, Tom kept pointing out an enormous tree that he wanted to take down. It turned out to be an engineering feat. The tree wanted to go down in the ravine; at that point, it's almost straight down 400 feet. But by using lines, walkie-talkies, and the tractor, we managed to drop it.

We worked until about 3:30 this afternoon. Then suddenly the wind came up and the ash blew down out of the trees, so we simply had to quit. Even with masks, it got in your eyes and stung like beach sand in a high wind hitting your face. It was a bright clear sky with the sun shining, but when the ash started blowing you couldn't see beyond the first row of trees. The big trees at Dorland's to the south just went out of sight. So we quit for a half hour until the wind went down. Then we went back to work.

Meanwhile, Nora was up washing the volcano ash off the roof so that, if the weather warmed up, she wouldn't have it all in the house. Pat cleaned the ash out of the gutters. When the wind changed, the temperature came up and the ash all dried. A 10 mph breeze means that you just can't see. We all wear masks outside and they fill up. The ash gets in your ears. It gets in your eyes. Your hair feels like it's full of beach sand. You can't even shave without washing two or three times because the ash fouls up the electric razor. Nora got the bulk of the stuff off the roof that had the downspouts and eaves all plugged up. We took off all the downspouts. One of the other interesting things was that Nora had taken the cover off the swimming pool the evening before the mountain erupted and now she has a swimming pool full of ash. We washed the road in front of our house, but the neighbors on either side didn't. So each vehicle that comes up the road leaves the area completely obscured from sight.

Due to the volcano, we have some new rules and regulations at the house now. There's a sign saying, "Use the back door only. Shake your clothes out. Take your shoes off and don't come in the house with them." The door leading into the utility room has a sign that says, "Please brush off your clothes outside and take your shoes off." We're serious about this ash. The vacuum cleaner won't keep up and brooms are no good.

When you think of "ash," you usually don't think of the heavy substance that's here. This is a mixture of brown and gray and also black colors. The local news says that, under a microscope, there are three different kinds of particles blown up by the volcano. It feels like gritty sand.

There's a new local ruling that the Sheriff's Department can arrest anyone going over 15 mph because it raises the dust. In the village, there's no way to clean the streets so every car that comes by makes a terrible amount of dust. Nora decided only to go to town in early morning, when there's dew and the damp means the dust doesn't get raised. If you go to the expressway, you have to wear a facemask even in the car because the dust is so granular that you don't want to breathe it. So the dust has really changed our way of living.

Pat was up cleaning gutters for the second time today. They got a wheelbarrow full off the south side of the house and another one off the east side. It will take another day's work just to get the downspouts back into operation. Nora used water to wash off her raspberry and blueberry plants because they were all hanging down to the ground. Cindy is picking strawberries. After the volcano erupted, there's been a lot of conversation about what to do with the strawberries fields, whether to wash them off or wait until the strawberries get to the processing plants.

Today is Father's Day. Nancy made me the most beautiful card for Grandfather's Day. Karen called and wished me "Happy Father's Day" and said I could come down to San Francisco where they don't have any ash. But I said I'd wait right here for her to come on up.

Last night Nancy and Amy (Nancy's friend) got me to convince her mother to let Amy stay in the trailer with her. It sounded like it would be at least an hour and a half of giggling, so I decided they could have the trailer and I'd sleep in Nancy's room. Today, Nancy had to go to town to an orthodontist and get wires on her teeth, but she's happy. Amy is going to stay with Nancy in the trailer tonight again and I'll have Nancy's room.

By the end of the week, I'll have completed the woodcutting. Then we're going to work in the field to the north where they have planted Christmas trees. We want to fence in above the trees. So that will be the next project.

Van (center) with Nora and Tom Malloy at the DC (Damn Cow) Ranch

CHAPTER EIGHTEEN

OUR ADVENTURES IN MEXICO
Luella M. Van Raalte

How it Started

Our interest in Mexico and helping children there began in 1962 when Van attended a Catholic "Cursillo" retreat in Saginaw, Michigan. In a 1975 interview with Prudy Mead for the *Leelanau Enterprise* Van explained, "Here's what a Cursillo is: you spend a weekend in a basement of a gymnasium, and you sleep on a lumpy cot. You listen to a ghetto priest who knows about poverty first hand. You think about what he's telling you. It gets into your brain and when they finally let you out of there, you've got a plan. You decide you're going to do something about poverty. You're going to help somebody! It wasn't until 1966 that I heard of a program called Youth for Understanding, but when I learned what it was all about, I decided this would be a great opportunity to put into practice what I experienced in that Saginaw basement. Luella and I wrote and explained we'd like to foster a Mexican exchange student, not one of those affluent types who usually get to come, but a person from the working class."

In December 1966 Maria Louisa Olvera Arrequin arrived at our home in Leland to stay with us for a semester and attend school at St. Mary's Lake Leelanau. We didn't know any Spanish, and her English was limited, so communication was challenging. But we found ways to understand each other and became very fond of her. We later learned that she was picked because we had asked for someone from the working class. She only found out shortly before the trip that she would be coming. We were certainly glad that we didn't get someone from a wealthy family in Mexico City who was used to having maid service. That happened to another family we knew and it wasn't a good experience for them.

Van, Maria and Luella in living room of 411 S. Main St. house

Trips to Cuidad Valles

Our time with Maria was so wonderful that we decided to visit her in her hometown of Cuidad Valles which is in the state of San Luis Potosi in the foothills of the Sierra Madres Mountains. To prepare, we took Spanish lessons from Eleanor Brakeman, a retired teacher who took great joy in her "senior" students.

In 1968 we made the first of many trips. We stayed in a small apartment at the Valles Hotel and made friends with the owners, the staff and other guests. Through Maria's parents we met Profesora Chuy Santana, the head of the Academia Comercial Potosina, a school for young people who have completed their secondary education. The students are educated to become bilingual and work in secretarial and accounting jobs.

Profesora Chuy Santana

As Van said in the *Enterprise* interview, "In a country like Mexico a school like this is a real opportunity. Here for as little as $20 a month we could get kids up and out of a life not worth talking about into an educational experience. I couldn't pass that up and neither could Luella." By paying for tuition at the Academia, we have helped many students over the years. We also helped children that we met through workers at the Valles Hotel in their studies at the regular schools.

Over the next two decades, we made many trips to Cuidad Valles. Whenever we arrived, word spread fast through the local grapevine that we were in town. Then a steady stream of visitors, including many of the students that we had sponsored, would stop by to visit. Some spoke excellent English and others spoke no

English at all. It gave our Spanish a good workout as we tried to converse. One day, Juan Martinez's mother came by to thank us for our help to Juan. She didn't speak English but with the help of others we were able to have a conversation with her. Her husband died two years ago of a heart attack leaving her with eleven children. Juan was the oldest and the youngest was seven months at the time. With our sponsorship, Juan finished at the Academy and now has a good job in Tampico with a radio station.

Maria married and has a little girl named Nancy and a son Sergio. There are 17 family members living in their three-room house. Getting to their house is a challenge as the roads in Valles are full of chuckholes, even in the downtown section, and some roads are passable only for a burro or on foot. Often we regretted our offer to drive anyone anywhere. Our Plymouth Barracuda sedan was not made for driving on those rutted streets.

Hotel Valles, Cuidad Valles, S.L.P., Mexico where Van & Luella stayed

We often went to Mass on Sunday at Maria's church downtown. Waiting outside for the previous Mass to end, we noted that all of the men removed their sombreros when they passed the church and the women made the sign of the cross when they passed by, even if they were in a car or bus. The church apparently at one time had a beautiful arched ceiling, but something must have happened as it is now gone and there are timbers crisscrossed supporting the roof. It gave one an eerie feeling. The church is about 100 feet in length but because of the side altars there is very limited seating and many are left standing. During the Mass we attended, one little girl about five or so must have gotten tired of standing so she walked up to the sanctuary and sat down on the bench usually reserved for the altar boys. She then proceeded to eat the bread that she had in her hand, picked up the crumbs, licked her fingers, then folded her arms and sat and listened. It was during the sermon and no one paid any attention to her.

Mountain Driving

The bad roads in town were nothing compared with the challenges of driving in the mountains. We particularly remember one trip from Cuidad Valles to Mexico City via the city of San Luis Potosi. It was a rainy, dark morning and we were not too happy about it, thinking of the mountainous road to San Luis Potosi. Had we known how bad it was, we would have worried more! We got under way and before long started climbing. It was still raining and the roads were slippery so progress was slow. We went up, up, up and around horseshoe bends. There were no guardrails, but steep drop-offs, and buses and trucks coming towards you were often in the center of the road. In several places the fog was so thick that it was possible to see only a few yards ahead. It was a nail-biting drive.

Eventually it stopped raining, the sun came out and we had magnificent views to enjoy. Another hazard of driving in Mexico, even on main roads, was that there were often cows or burros on the road. In one spot on this trip we had to stop as there were two burros in the middle of the road and a man was trying to pull them off, but they were stubborn and braced their legs and pulled back. 'Twas easy to see where the phrase "stubborn as a jackass" originated! We laughed and took a couple of pictures. Finally we arrived at San Luis Potosi. Gracias Dios! It took us six hours to go 165 miles.

Van's stay at a Ranch

On one of our trips, we met the Graves family who had a ranch and they extended an invitation to visit them. Van decided to take them up on the invitation and he was as excited as a kid for the chance to be a cowboy for a week. He got a new pair of cowboy boots, a sombrero, denims and a belt. The directions to get there were not simple. "Drive from Valles to Antiquo Morelos, about forty miles, then to Nuevo Morelos, cross a bridge, go one kilometer, go past three thatched huts and some palm trees, then turn left, go through a village and at the church at the top of a knoll you keep left." At the first gate on the ranch a bunch of kids came out to open it and Van threw them some centavos.

After going through the second gate, Van stopped the car, went up to two men who were arc welding and asked "Que esta senor Graves casa?" One of the men in perfect English said, "Oh, it's right over there, just below the hill." It took Van so by surprise because the old man who spoke was exceptionally dark for a Mexican and yet he had no trace of an accent. It turns out that this man worked for Graves for a month before Graves knew that he spoke English. He let Graves stumble through broken Spanish and undoubtedly enjoyed it immensely.

The hacienda is on a foothill on a slope of the western mountain range, and the view is magnificent. One can see twenty thousand acres of ranch land from there. The water at the ranch comes from a spring in the mountains and is excellent for drinking.

That afternoon, Mr. Graves asked Van if he wanted to ride a horse and pointed out a horse tied to a tree. That horse, Van discovered, had never been ridden. Perhaps they were hoping to have a little amusement at the gringo's expense? Van quickly made known the fact that he was looking for a gentle old horse. So they gave him an old hag that he called "Lop Ears." The only way to make him go was to boot him in the ribs with both feet.

The next day Van went out with a fence crew. The cowboys took off into the palm brush but Van stayed on the road because many of the bushes have inch long needles. The cowboys wear leather chaps and they all carry machetes on their saddles. All of a sudden there was a commotion around the fence crew. Van soon saw the reason for it, three wild pigs. The crew had two dogs and the dogs went after the pigs. In the next hour the cowboys killed all three pigs with their machetes. Wild pigs are vicious and they have sharp tusks. One of them gored a dog in the jaw. The crew had wild pig for breakfast the next day, prepared only as a Mexican ranch cook can prepare it. Van said it was delicious!

The wild pig on its way to the cookhouse

After taking a day off to just rest and take pictures, Van got back on old Lop Ears to deliver food to the crews. That day the caballeros gave Van some palm nuts to eat. The nut with the covering is about the size of a golf ball. You break it open between two rocks. The nut itself is about the size of a chickpea and tastes like a walnut. He also tried heart of palm and a "chote" which looks like a cucumber and is sweet. You don't eat it; you suck the juice from it.

Van had a wonderful time at the ranch. I was glad to have him back, but I kept him at arm's length until he shed his flea and tick infested clothes!

Van at the ranch

Luella, La Profesora

The variety of contacts that we have made in previous visits provided us lots of interesting experiences in Mexico. While Van was at the ranch, I was asked to teach several English classes by Silvia Ruelas at the Institute in El Centro. She took me first to her third year English class. She said I should tell them about Leland, our boat trip or anything, so I talked to them as well as showing pictures of Leland. Then I asked if they had any questions and their questions were "What is your name?" "Do you have any children?" etc. etc. I did the same thing for the class in first year English but they did not ask many questions since most of them were unsure of their English. Then I went to the adult English class. This class was composed one doctor, several teachers, office workers (one, Josephina, from the Valles Hotel). They asked many questions and I felt very much at ease with them. I thoroughly enjoyed every minute of the three hours.

A Visit to the Local Prison

One of Van's enlightening experiences was to go with Profesora Santana to visit a local prison where some of the students at the Academy are teaching the inmates job skills such as typing. Later Van said that all one has read and heard about the horrors of Mexican jails are true. There are about 150 men in the jail ranging from 12 years to 80. There were web cots for about 80 men and the rest slept on the hard, bumpy cement floor. Each gets two pesos a day for food. If the family of the prisoner brings food to him he might have enough, otherwise he would starve. There was a big dark hole at one end. No need to ask where the urinal was as it could be smelled the minute one entered the door of the jail. Van had been told by someone once, "If you land in jail while you are in Mexico, for whatever reason and guilty or not, buy your way out!" At the time he thought it was preposterous advice but now he knows it is justified.

A Surprise Celebration

Over the years we have assisted over a dozen young people in Valles, helping them to receive an education. This education is both in the federal schools and in the Academia Potosi. One day Prof. Chuy asked us to be at the Academy at 9:30. When we arrived all of the students were seated on chairs in groups. We were escorted by Prof. Chuy to a platform while drums and a trumpet played. Then a corsage was pinned on me. An English student announced that a program had been planned in our honor. Five girls dressed in Hawaiian costumes did a hula dance. Another group did a typical Mexican dance. Two students played guitars and sang. A boy and a girl did an Indian dance and then another couple did a Spanish dance in which the girl held a rose in her mouth with the stem extending. The boy had to get the rose by the stem with his teeth and at no time interrupt the rhythm of the dance. The last song was sung by a young man who imitated a famous Mexican singer and the crowd of kids went wild! One of the girls presented a bouquet of gladiolas to him, and as he was finishing his song, he walked over and presented them to me.

Van chickened out when it came time for a thank you speech and let me have the honor. Speech making is not his cup of tea. I don't mind as long as I don't have time to worry about it beforehand. There was an official photographer there who took a picture of me with my arms stretched out in a big thank you gesture! This was the first time in our lives that we ever had so much publicity and honor. Needless to say we were overwhelmed with the kindness and generosity of our friends. It took a lot of work to organize a program like this and we all enjoyed every minute of it.

Luella and Van (second and third from left) in official photograph of Luella's thank you speech

CHAPTER NINETEEN

LETTERS FROM LUELLA: 1971-83
Luella M. Van Raalte

Editor's Note: These are excerpts from letters that Luella wrote to family members.

Holding the Home Front for Van's Garage

I have to stay within earshot of the phone because both Van and John are away. And although the shop is theoretically closed, because of AAA, we have to be available for service calls. Now, I'm not going to take the wrecker out on a service call, but Jimmy Schlueter is available to do that; however, I would have to go pound on his door since he doesn't have a telephone! I had to go out to the shop to rent bikes to 4 girls from Traverse. We had promised to do that.

A Visit from JP & Donna

Tonight JP and Donna were here after school and for supper. I like having them around. Donna wanted me to sit next to her and watch her color. She does do a very nice job. JP is such a tease. Tonight was joke night again, and here are a couple that he sprang on us:

    JP: What is black and white and red all over?
    Grandparents, simultaneously: A newspaper!
    JP: No, a zebra with a diaper rash! (giggling loudly)
    J: What has six legs, two heads, and one tail?
    Gs: We give up.
    JP: A man on a horse.

JP gets such a charge out of telling jokes and his giggling is infectious. With someone like him around, the world takes on brighter and happier tones.

Disappearing Cigars

Van likes to smoke cigars. Christine and JP are determined to show him the error of his ways. When they find his cigars, they hide them. Once they took out the batteries from his flashlight and put the cigars there. Another time they froze them in an ice cube tray. Luckily Van buys cheap cigars and is amused by the kids' antics. They also drew a cartoon explaining why he should quit. He framed it to show his appreciation of the artwork and humor. But he hasn't given up his cigars.

A House Full of Rosie's Friends

This is the weekend that Rosie's Oakland University friends are visiting. We have three cots in the living room, two in the tent outside, and the upstairs is FULL. They are a good bunch of kids and we are enjoying them. This morning Van took a group out sailing, but a couple of them were novice sailors and they didn't "HIKE" backwards when they were supposed to, so the boat went over. So far, they have gone through 3 cases of coke, 10 pounds of chicken, hot dogs, buns, 4 dozen sweet rolls, 10 pounds of hamburger, plus misc. other food. After they leave, I will be in a whirlwind of preparation for Nora's arrival. In the meantime, I've been substituting for Rosie at the shop. On Thursday I worked at Joyce of Leland because her regular bookkeeper quit. And, oh yes, David Kleis, the former art student, is around town and asked to have a small space in the refrigerator to keep his food. He comes in and goes out, we're not sure where he's staying to sleep, but there's no room here! Right now, David is here studying, and we are both enjoying some NY cream sherry. Time now to stop and start some chili and strawberry shortcake for the gang!

Luella in kitchen of 411 S. Main St. house

Van's Snowmobiling on the "Go Dad Go"

Jack and Doe Schurman, Van and John went out snowmobiling on Saturday. About 5 p.m. Van came home and went upstairs to lie down. Then John called to ask how he was. John told me that Van's machine had tipped over on the ice and threw him off and they found him out cold on the ice. They helped him get up and he brushed them away and said "Leave me alone!" but promptly fell down again. So they got him on the machine and he headed for home. He parked his machine at the garage, got into the pickup and drove home. When I asked Van why he didn't tell me all this, he was utterly amazed. He didn't remember a thing about it. The last thing he actually remembered when he woke up was flying through the air on the ice. When he came downstairs, he looked out to see where the snowmobile was because he didn't remember how he got home. Fortunately, he had a helmet on and it got dented instead of his head.

Van on his "Go Dad Go" snowmobile

Keeping Things

I'm still fighting overpopulation of things. Being a sentimentalist, I just can't throw away anything that has any memory attached to it; being somewhat thrifty, I can't throw out anything that has any value. My solution is to put it in the attic until later. Soon the attic will also be bulging!

Social Security - and Dentures

What a day! My social security check came this morning for $1,313.10. I've never had that much money at one time in my life and to think I had to retire to have it happen. I'm putting most of it in savings for a trip to Washington DC and also to Oregon and then I'll be able to pay for my new dentures. I was beginning to worry about paying for that. And there is a story about the dentures!

Last Saturday, I had gone to Traverse and when I got back, I was tired and frustrated. It was very dreary out...and I was hungry. So stupidly, I drank more sherry than I should have. After we had eaten I suddenly realized that I had better lie down. I went to sleep, but then woke up feeling sick. It was hard walking down the hall because the walls seemed to want to close in on me. But I made it to the bathroom in time. Then I felt much better, but after I got back to bed my mouth felt funny. Suddenly I was WIDE-awake! I had actually flushed my upper dentures down the toilet. Luckily, I have my old dentures from 1935. So I put them in and didn't say a word to Van. He would NEVER let me forget about it. Then he noticed after a few days (the teeth in the old pair look different) and I casually replied that I was having some trouble - which I was because the old and new dentures don't mesh well. Since then he hasn't said anything else. So I am having my fun along with the discomfort!

LWV Budgets - and Sherry Cake

Tomorrow night I have a LWV budget meeting here. We will chase figures into the right places, but first we have to estimate how much income there will be. I was budget chairman last year also, but don't want to do it next year. We will start the meeting tomorrow night with dessert and coffee. I plan to make a cake that is a 3-layer yellow cake with each layer punched with holes and a 1/4-cup of sherry poured over it.

Pat Malloy and the Train East

Pat came back from Oregon with us on the train. He had a good time on the train ride east. He traversed it from end to end at least 20 times a day. He knew almost all of the passengers, and occasionally when Van would go looking for him for lunch or something, someone would say "You looking for Pat? He went that way." Everyone knew Pat. He had his picture taken with two Japanese models by the Japanese Press. They were doing a fashion book on American people and got off at Banff, much to his regret. They gave him some Japanese money that he treasures.

Luella's Schedule while Van is in Hospital: Drinks with Charley

Did I tell you about my busy schedule? Van was in the hospital. I was going in to see him daily as well as working a couple of hours at Van's Garage and also at the Joyce of Leland dress shop and we had art students (Audrey Olson, Lanene Smith, Jerry Cantania and David Kleis) staying here. I made a daily schedule for myself so I wouldn't forget something special or important and had left it on the dining room table. The four were sitting at the table in my absence and Jerry happened to look at the schedule and said he exclaimed, "Look at this. Mama Van doesn't even have a half hour to spare. We've got to get some relaxation in there somewhere."

So, they put in "Drinks with Charley" on the schedule wherever they found a break, even if it was midnight! I discovered it the next day and chuckled, and then decided to have a little fun. So I took the schedule in to Van at the hospital and said, "This is what I do every day." He read it through and when he came to the "Drinks with Charley," he said "What the hell is this?" So, we all had some fun out of it.

Summer Visitors

We always have lots of visitors in the summer. Jinny and family and two friends are coming up this weekend. Sunday is the annual dinner at St. Mary's so I'll have to work part of the day. Van will take anyone interested out fishing in the Hall's boat as the Seabee is having some work done. Marie will stay for the following week. Karen will be up during the week and Rosie and Mark are coming the following weekend. After they leave, Audrey Olson (who is staying here for the whole summer) and I will whisk the sheets off and fresh ones back on because three photography students will be coming for two weeks. To add to the chaos, our 10-year old washer and dryer went out of commission. Van got parts today and is repairing them. Johnnie Suelzer wants to come up on August 19th, but he may have to sleep in the boat!

Losing Weight

By the way, I've lost six pounds since we returned from Oregon, the hard way, just plain sensible eating and NO SHERRY. We do have a low-alcohol table wine with dinner. I'm short and small-boned so the 126 pounds I weighed made me look a bit tubby. Thought I had better do something after Van suggested that maybe I should go to Weight Watchers, and that he would pay the fee and give me $100 if I lost 10 pounds! I told him I appreciated his concern for my health and looks, but I would just use my will power, and I didn't want his d@#n bribe money! My Swedish temper got riled up and I missed out on some easy money. He's a nice guy and means well, and I really love him, but there are times when I could wring his neck!

At Home While Van is Working on the Malloy Ranch

I have been working on my Spanish. My teacher Eleanor Brakeman and I meet twice a week and I'm translating letters as both Francisco and Prof. Santana write in Spanish. Prof. Santana's typed letters are easier to translate. Francisco writes in long hand, which is difficult to read.

Tomorrow I will do the bookwork at Joyce of Leland's and in the evening we have our first book club meeting at Helen Lindquist's. Then there is a Day of Recollection at Maple City that I have registered for. I've also been driving Mrs. Bowen and her sister to doctor appointments, etc. Last Saturday morning I got an urgent call to take her sister to LMH at Northport. She is 85 and very fragile. I got her there in good time.

The Burglar in the Basement

The night before Van got home from Portland, Oregon, I woke up with a start at 4:30 a.m. I heard a crash downstairs and thought that maybe someone was breaking in. There have been a number of break-ins around the area and since it was the week John and Jan were in Kentucky, I had all of the shop money here. I listened and tiptoed to the head of the stairs but heard nothing further. However, I was not brave enough to venture downstairs, so I got Van's trusty 22 rifle out of the clothes closet and laid it on the bed by my side and went back to sleep. The gun isn't loaded but would be useful in conking someone over the head if necessary!

When I got downstairs in the morning, our cat Tony was waiting patiently to be fed, but Black Mama Kitty was nowhere in sight. Presently I heard a faint "meow." She had gotten locked in the basement overnight, and in her attempts to get out, she had knocked over a box of empty cat food tins on the top step. The cans had rolled down the steps and all over the basement floor. That was the answer to "What was the crash in the night?" I was glad that it was the night *before* Van came home and not the night after he left. I didn't really mind being alone, but this old house has lots of noises and creaks, especially when the wind blows.

Diocesan Council of Catholic Women

This past Thursday there was a DCCW workshop at Cadillac. This year I am again the International Affairs Commission Chairman for the Gaylord DCCW, so last Sunday I made a poster depicting the main points of the program for this year and also prepared folders for the regional chairmen. At the board meeting last August, we decided to have outside speakers. I thought I was going to have an easy time and just listen to the speakers. On Tuesday, however, I received a letter from the DCCW chairman asking me to take over the workshop. This meant preparing material for about a half-hour discussion that would happen five times. I did have ample material, so I prepared a general outline, and wasn't even nervous. I'm not taking credit for this, because I prayed very hard that I would forget about myself and think only of being able to bring something of value to the listeners. There were questions, so actually the time wasn't long enough.

Oregon Trip with the Texas Cowboy!

The job this trip was fence building. At first there was a lot of rain and getting trees out of the forest was a problem, but then the weather turned warm and sunny, so the fence building went well. Nora worked like a man right alongside of Van. She has strong muscles, but was getting very tired by the end.

I helped by doing secretarial tasks, cooking, canning, gardening, cleaning or whatever. Nora and Tom own three houses that they rent and are very involved in the Beefalo projects, [crossbreeding domestic cattle with American buffalo] so Nora has a lot of bookkeeping to keep accounts straight for Uncle Sam. In all this, she still manages to take guitar lessons.

While in Oregon, Van really enjoyed riding horses with Cindy and he bought a black cowboy hat. This raised the question of how to pack it for the trip home. So he wore it. At O'Hare airport a little boy pointed at Van and said to his mom, "Look at the Texas cowboy, Mom." Van was wearing black slacks and a black and white checked jacket and looked right sharp!

Library Work

I volunteer a half-day a week at the Leland Library cataloguing books. I can do from 30 to 35 books in an afternoon. In March Azalia Bishop asked me to be the Secretary for the Friends of the Library. Standing in front of people has always bothered me, and makes me more nervous as I grow older, so I told her that I had decided not to take any more "face the people" jobs. But I also told her that work behind the scenes didn't faze me, so I'm now typist for the group and enjoying it. This, plus the Spanish lessons, and my DCCW work seems to keep me busy. I'm also chairman of the Library Volunteers. People have to be contacted as to when they would like to work and a schedule drawn up.

The Back Yard and the Seabee

Did I tell you that the huge storage building next to us on Main Street has been taken down? The Stander Marine building down the block has been made into offices and stores. But now the Seabee in our side yard with its white canvas cover stands out like a sore thumb, and every bit of backyard clutter (of which there is plenty) shows up clearly. If Van is true to his Keeler blood, he will want to move to a more uncivilized area.

Winter Day with Projects

Van and Ozzie Cordes are building cupboards for tools at Van's Garage. John told me a while back that when he wants something done, he talks about doing it himself in a conversation with Van. Then sometime later Van comes up with the idea in a little different form and offers to do it. This had better be a part of the letter that Van doesn't read!

I usually shudder when Van says, "Could you give me a few minutes of your valuable time?" I am always happy to be of help, but sometimes I sure don't like the job! One day I helped him clean the creosote out of the basement stove pipes; they were clogged and that is dangerous. Then I helped Van build a new clothes chute, which necessitated taking the washbowl out of the upstairs bathroom so that he could repair the water leak that had rotted the previous chute. I never know whether I am going to be a chimney sweep's helper, a mechanic's helper, a plumber's helper or what.

The banks of snow by the Merc are 8 to 10 feet high. They have shoveled two walks to get in the front of the store and when one drives out the parking lot, as I had to do today, one has to stick the nose of the car out very cautiously. We have had four blizzards on four consecutive weekends. I haven't driven to Mass for 3 weeks.

Head Honcho for the Seabees

Van is the "Head Honcho" for the Michigan, Indiana and Kentucky WWII Seabees from the 129th Battalion. A Honcho's job is to write letters to the men in his district with news or whatever. Van is writing about his experiences in the Seabees. I am glad he is doing this. He puts on tape what he wants to write, then I type it out and we go over it together. I take out most of the "hells" and "damns," then I type the final version, get copies made, and address and send out the envelopes. There are 32 men in this district, so it does take time.

Moving from the Old House

Remember that poem "There is a porpoise close behind me and he's treading on my tail"? Well that is the way I feel, only it is not a porpoise, it's Van. He is anxious to get moved into the new house [103 Oak St., Leland] and he keeps pushing me to do this, that, and the other thing. He already has his bed and chest over there. Last night he and JP took the hutch over, in the morning he took the desk, and tonight he took the TV. He moves the big things but I have all of the small household items, books, etc. to pack...and to decide what goes and what gets tossed.

Nora painting at Oak Street house

Nora finished the painting at the new house before she left. We had decided on a rusty red for the shutters and roof trim and it dresses the house up. Van was going to paint the shutters green, but Nora asked me what color I wanted and I thought rusty red would be a good contrast. She liked that too so she talked him into that color. Nora also suggested making a half circle drive in front of the house with flowers along the edge. Then people will come to the front door when they visit. I think we'll do that.

The remodeling in the new house will cost about $6,000 by the time we're finished. Van is working on a carport for the Rambler and we have made 19 storm windows. Our new neighbors have been coming over with apples, tomatoes, squash etc.... and some delicious rolls.

103 Oak St., Leland, MI where Van & Luella moved in 1983

Family Genealogy

Helen Juilleret is working on the genealogy of the Nelson family. Yesterday we went to the Courthouse here to try to find out where my grandfather, Christian Neidecker, was buried. He died January 18, 1894, at the age of 68 in Leelanau Township. I remember my mother telling me that her father lived with her sister, Emma Brown, in Omena. He was born in Eichstetten, Germany, as was his wife. I've never been very interested in genealogy, but Helen has been. I remember my father singing Swedish songs, but you know how kids are. I just wasn't very interested in information on Sweden.

St. Mary's Dinner and Lemon Pies ... at 77

Today is St. Mary's Annual chicken dinner and it was pouring rain. I went to 8:00 Mass and took the lemon pies. A kind gentleman helped me carry them into the hall. I am on Bingo prizes, and don't need to go back until 3 p.m. but I decided to chicken out. Between the rain and the Sunday afternoon summer traffic, I decided that a 77-year-old woman could stay home. IF the bingo is actually happening in the rain, I'm sure someone will help.

Editors Note: Following is an excerpt from the last letter Luella wrote to Sara. It was written in 1990 when Luella was 81, never mailed, but discovered later. By this point, Luella's memory loss was very noticeable. Yet, the letter shows the generous spirit of wanting to share love that was a really deep quality in Luella.

I am sorry not to be with Van at the Seabee reunion, which I have always enjoyed. But my arthritic hip put an end to it this year. I am happy that Jinny is going with Van, as it will be good for him to get away from everyday life and see Seabee pals again. I do think of Nora and Tom often and wish their children lived near so I could be of help to them. [Nora and Tom had died in a boating accident in Mexico in January 1990.] Well, the phone just rang and an old friend is coming, so this is it for now. Am looking forward to seeing you soon. Love, Mother. Love to all. Love to all. Mother.

The family gathers for John & Luella's 50th wedding anniversary celebration in 1983
Standing: Karen, Rosie, John D., Jinny, Sara and Nora
Seated: Luella and Van.

CHAPTER TWENTY

BOATING AT 80: SEPTEMBER 1988

John K. Van Raalte

Lou Raynor's sailboat

I want to tell you about a little boat trip that my grandson JP and I took in September of my 80th year. Lou Raynor, a retired university sculptor, had a cottage on South Manitou and a 24-foot sailboat he agreed to loan to us. On the day we planned to leave, the wind was blowing about 30 mph. A couple boats about our size left the harbor and seemed to be going more up and down then forward. But we thought that the wind was going to die, so we decided we would leave that afternoon. I'd never sailed on this boat and JP had never sailed at all, so we had to look over the rigging and figure it out. We left the Leland Harbor about noon. JP was navigator and cook on the trip.

After we got through the waves right against the Leland harbor seawall, it smoothed out a little and we hoisted the sails, shut off the outboard, and off we went. We had foul weather gear on as we got a lot of splashing over the edge. It should have taken us about three hours to North Manitou, but it took us five. We didn't know much about sailing this boat and we were also headed directly into the wind. I could run my scow about 22 degrees into the wind, but we could only manage about 40 degrees into the wind on this one. We got to North Manitou and tied up at the Forest Service dock. Then we toured that part of the island on foot. JP hadn't been there before; I had been there many times with Pete Jurica on the logging barge. We tried to sleep, but the boat would bump against the dock and wake us up, so we had to move out and drop anchor.

Van on boat, Doris Shirk on dock at Beaver Island

Next day we set sail for North Fox Island. There are no docks, so we had to examine the rocky bottom to find out where we thought an anchor would hold.

Our next destination was Beaver Island. We experimented with the sails and got so that we could go with a pretty good speed and we had good wind. It's a narrow maneuver to get into that harbor and you don't have space for tacking, so we dropped sails and used our outboard.

We looked up Doris Shirk, who used to live on South Manitou. She has a store with a little restaurant downtown. She took us on a 16-mile tour of the island in her old battered pickup, telling us about the farms and the history. That night, trying to sleep, JP and I kept hearing little tap-tap-taps on the side of the boat. We got up and found it was a group of ducks who kept tapping, hoping that we'd come out with some food. We didn't, so they finally left.

Van at helm with Beaver Island in the distance

While we were on Beaver Island, I called home. You can use your marine radio and hook into the system at Charlevoix, and I got John on the line. I remembered that once I'd left Wisconsin without telling anyone there that we were leaving or anyone in Michigan that we were headed across and when we hit heavy seas and the engine died, we were sitting out in Lake Michigan without a radio. I decided then that I'd never do that again.

The next day we headed north and planned to come down the west side of the island. We got north all right, but then the wind died and we could only make about a mile and a half an hour. We had only one small tank for the outboard, so we couldn't motor the rest of the way. We had a depth finder, so we dropped anchor and spent the night there.

Overnight the wind changed directions, blowing out of northeast to south. We planned to head home to Leland, but the wind was gusting up to about 40 mph. We picked up a cross sea because of the changing wind and took some water into the cockpit. We went about another 15 minutes before we concluded that we weren't getting where we needed to go. We headed instead for the north side of the Fox Islands. The seas were big enough that when we dropped down between waves the islands went out of sight.

Waves like these dropped a "washtub" of water in the boat

We made good time, and we picked out a place off South Fox to anchor. We put out a few fish lines, but we didn't catch anything.

At 1:24 a.m. we woke up hearing the wind whistling through the rigging and it sounded like a hurricane. JP. said, "Well, what do you think, Grandpa?" I said, "Well, as near as I can tell, we haven't moved. As long as the anchor is holding, we should go back to sleep." Neither one of us woke up until after 7 a.m. We had a dinghy and went ashore to look at how the sea was on the east side. We figured that if we waited until 10 a.m., we could make a run into Leland. It was choppy when we started out, then the wind started decreasing and we motored the last half-mile into Leland because the wind died out.

I can truthfully say that this was an absolutely marvelous trip! I had wanted for years to make a sailboat trip on Lake Michigan. We made it, and it was exciting enough to be interesting. JP said, "There are very few 80 year old men who go boating around Lake Michigan on a sailboat." Amen!

EPILOGUE

In 1983 Van and Luella's family hosted a 50th wedding anniversary party for them. Those attending were asked to contribute to a "Memory Book." Dr. John Suelzer, a lifelong close friend of Van and Luella, wrote a piece, excerpted below, that is a fitting close for this book of stories.

> *"Maureen and I well remember the long kitchen talks, the cinnamon rolls, mason jars, good breakfasts and the love of good friends. We will never forget the living example of God's way – two people of modest means and many responsibilities who helped so many people less fortunate than themselves. I guess the Suelzers never could and never will forget Van and Luella. You made us all better people because we knew you."*

In 1984, when she was 75, Luella showed the first signs of dementia and began a steady decline into Alzheimer's. Van took care of her at home for six years. In 1989, major heart surgery pushed her further into dementia, followed by the sorrow of the death of their daughter, Nora, and her husband, Tom, on New Year's Day, 1990. In August 1990, when she no longer recognized her surroundings as home, the family moved her to the Northport Long-Term Care Center where she received excellent care until her death in June 1998 at the age of 89. Van visited Luella every day of her stay at Northport until he gave up driving and moved to Bob and Fran Jelinek's small family-run assisted living home among the cherry orchards in Gills Pier, north of Leland. Van passed away in November 2004 at the age of 96.

This book of stories provides a legacy for two unique individuals who lived life to the fullest and enriched the lives of family and friends.

Made in the USA
Monee, IL
30 January 2020